×××××××××××××××××××××××××××××××××××

cross stitch

miniatures

×××××××××××××××××××××××××××××××××××

cross stitch

miniatures

fransie snyman ×××××××××××××××××××××××××××××

Author's acknowledgements

I would like to thank everybody who showed such interest and gave such wonderful support while I was writing and doing the embroidery for this book. Thank you Rita, Irmia, Diane, Teniel, Rhona, Melindie, Lynette, Francia, Nikki, Wilsia and Estie for assistance with the embroidery. Thank you Colré and Francia for your great ideas. To Paul, Wilsia and Ludaan – many thanks for all your help in putting together the advent calendar.

Thank you Lindie for allowing us free rein in your home to take the photographs, and for providing such delicious refreshments!

Thank you Wilsia of Metz Press for your patience, support and encouragement.

Thanks to our Heavenly Father for talents and wonderful opportunities.

Published by Metz Press
1 Cameronians Avenue
Welgemoed, 7530
South Africa

First published in 2006
Copyright © Metz Press 2006
Text and patterns copyright © Fransie Snyman
Photographs copyright © Metz Press

Publisher and editor	Wilsia Metz
Design and lay-out	Lindie Metz
Translation	Retha Venter
Photographer	Thomas Mihal
Reproduction	Cape Imaging Bureau, Cape Town

Printed and bound in China by WKT Company Ltd
ISBN   1-919992-26-X

Contents

Introduction

Do you often want to embroider, but you don't have the time to tackle large projects that would take months to complete? We live in busy times, with everybody always rushing off to some appointment or meeting, or to get our children to sports practice or other activities in time. At the end of a long day we then feel utterly frustrated because it seems as though we didn't get to do anything productive.

Cross-stitch embroidery is a therapeutic and relaxing hobby, and with miniature cross-stitch patterns you can produce something original in no time at all. All the patterns can be worked in a few hours and the projects needn't cost you an arm and a leg. The embroidery is small enough to take along wherever you go, so you can spend time between tasks happily stitching away.

If you sometimes feel frustrated because of all the time you lose while waiting, you can now put it to good use by working a stitch or two. Think of all the times you sit waiting at your kids' hockey, netball and rugby practice or music and ballet classes. Most of the patterns are so easy that you can even work while watching your favourite soapies on television.

You can also combine the motifs for larger projects, but because you stitch them one at a time, the project will be completed before you know it and you will never feel overwhelmed.

Alternative ideas for the use of patterns are given, as well as instructions for the completion of projects. Completing some of the projects requires basic sewing skills for which I do not give instructions. However, the sewing is basic and will most probably not be a problem.

You will also note that trimmings such as beads, charms, beady eyes, lace, paper flowers and buttons were used for many of the projects. Give your imagination free reign and use what you have. Where you would normally use a French knot, you can use a bead in the specific colour instead. In the simple motifs for children's rooms and articles, moving eyes are very effective.

It is sometimes difficult to work rounded shapes, especially flowers, in cross stitch. An easy solution is to use paper or silk flowers in your embroidery instead of stitches. With miniature cross-stitch projects it is also sometimes difficult to embroider small animals or shapes. In these cases charms come in handy.

One of the greatest benefits of cross-stitch embroidery is its versatility. So change and combine patterns and motifs to you heart's desire and give these projects your personal touch.

Materials

For cross-stitch embroidery you don't need much more than a needle and thread, and something to embroider on, be it fabric or any other material. However, the correct combination of these items to achieve a specific look, determines the success of your project.

Dedicated tools, such as a hoop, will also make things much easier.

Fabric

There are different kinds of fabric used specifically for cross-stitch embroidery, making your work much easier because of the holes into which you stitch.

AIDA

This is an excellent cotton basket-weave fabric, available in different counts. Aida's basket-weave is the best fabric for beginners.

The count represents the number of strands per inch (2,5 centimetres) and determines the size of the embroidery, as well as the thickness of the thread you should use. The lower the count, the fewer stitches per centimetre are worked. For fine, delicate embroidery you will therefore use a higher count fabric.

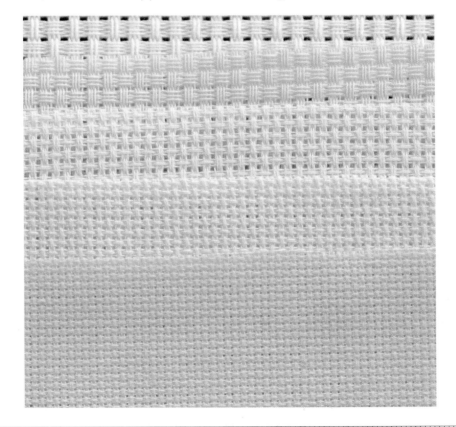

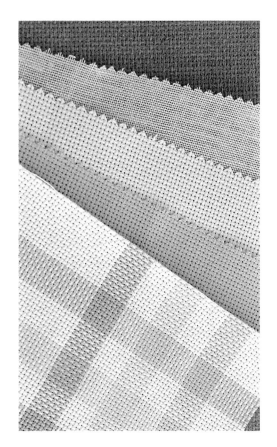

Aida is usually available in different colours and counts from 6 to 18. The 6-count is excellent to teach children to do cross-stitch embroidery, but it is not readily available. You will need 14-count for most of the projects in this book, as it is the most popular choice for beginners as well as experienced embroiderers.

FINISHED AIDA STRIPS

Aida is also available in ready to use strips of different widths, colours and counts, finished with a border pattern. These strips are especially suited to decorate face cloths, towels and serviettes, and can even be used for a border pattern on clothing items. You can also use them for bookmarks.

CUSTOM-MADE ITEMS WITH AIDA STRIPS

Custom-made items with woven sections of Aida, such as placemats, napkins, dish-cloths, towels, facecloths and baby bibs are available from most needlework and cross-stitch shops. Although the actual embroidery fabric is fairly expensive, these items are less expensive, because they are usually not entirely made up of basket-weave fabric. I used placemats with an Aida border for the napery project (see page 75), and a baby bib for the nursery project. Using these items saves a lot of time, as you don't have to make them up after completing the embroidery.

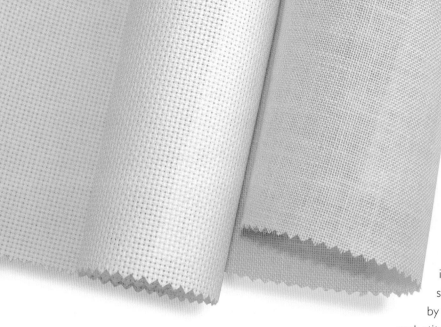

EVEN-WEAVE

This kind of fabric is also ideal for cross-stitch embroidery. The fabric is woven with the same number of threads horizontally and vertically. It is therefore easy to count the holes and to keep the stitches the same size. It is finer than Aida and makes for an end-product that looks more sophisticated.

Even-weave is also chosen according to the count, but the number of stitches per centimetre is determined by the number of strands over which each stitch is worked. For instance, if you work on 28-count and each stitch is worked over two strands, the size of the stitches will be the same as when you use 14-count Aida. The benefit of even-weave is that it is much easier to work fractional stitches. With fractional stitches it is possible to make rounded shapes and achieve a finer finish.

WASTE CANVAS

Waste canvas enables you to do cross-stitch embroidery on any fabric. It is a loosely woven, gauze-like fabric, available in different counts and, like Aida, determines the size and position of your stitches. It is basted onto the article to be embellished with embroidery and removed once you have completed the embroidery.

PLASTIC CANVAS

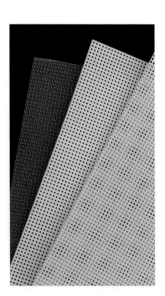

Plastic canvas is especially suited to cross-stitch embroidery for functional items, such as bookmarks, or to build three-dimensional shapes, such as trinket boxes, to decorate with embroidery. It is available in 14-count white and transparent plastic. Fractional stitches can't be worked on it and the background is mostly filled in completely to hide any finishing.

PERFORATED PAPER

Perforated 14-count paper is available in different colours for cross-stitch embroidery. It is especially suitable for cards, bookmarks, gift tags, Christmas-tree decorations and photo frames. The paper retains its shape and, because it does not fray, you don't have to worry about finishing off frayed edges. It is easy to cut decorative edges out of perforated paper. Using it for this purpose was very popular in the Victorian age.

Embroidery yarns

There is a large variety of embroidery yarns available for cross-stitch embroidery, and new products are released all the time. Most embroidery yarns are mercerised cotton, but unmercerised yarns such as *Coton à broder* are also available.

Mercerising is a finishing process during which the cotton fibres are treated in such a way that it swells to form a more rounded fibre. This fibre is up to 20% stronger and has a beautiful sheen.

Mercerising also improves the absorption of dyes by the fibres. The colours of mercerised cottons are therefore usually brighter.

STRANDED COTTON

Cross-stitch embroidery is usually done with stranded cotton. These yarns consist of 6 strands of mercerised cotton and are sold in lenghts of 8 metres. The number of strands used when you work, is determined by the count of the fabric you use. If you are unsure about how many strands to use, remove one strand of the fabric that you are going to use and make sure that the strand of yarn is of the same thickness. The following table can be used:

Count	Strands
11	4 to 6
14	2 to 3
16	2
18	1 to 2

For back stitching, use one less strand than for the cross stitches.

COTON À BRODER

This is flat, unmercerised cotton that is not readily available. It is spun to a single strand and is not meant to be divided. It is available in a reasonable variety of colours and adds a soft, matt finish to your embroidery. Unfortunately it shows dust much easier than the shinier stranded cotton.

SILK STRING COTTON

Silk string cotton is mercerised and has a beautiful silky lustre. It is availbale in strings as well as wound strands. It is fairly expensive and not very easy to work with, as the fine fibres tend to catch on one's skin, nails and the fabric. However, when you combine it with fine fabric, the end result is really something rather special.

PEARLISED COTTON

This single-wound, high-gloss yarn is available in a large variety of colours and three weights, namely 5, 8 and 20. The higher the number, the thinner the thread. The weight is chosen according to the count of the fabric.

Count	Number
11	5
14–16	8
18	20

SPECIAL AND DECORATIVE YARNS

For some of the projects in this book I used special stranded cotton yarns. Both DMC and Anchor have beautiful multi-coloured stranded yarns. Each strand consists of various shades of a colour, often combined with white.

Rayon stranded yarn has a beautiful sheen and looks like silk.

Metallic yarns are available in a large variety of colours and are ideal to embroider Christmas motifs or motifs for special occasions such as weddings, christenings or birthdays.

Because metallic yarns consist of very fine filaments they fray very easily. Dip the ends into clear nail varnish to prevent fraying. Work with shorter lenghts of yarn, preferably pushing the needle through one hole at a time while you are working. Push the needle through from front to back and again from back to front. Don't try to work both in and out in one movement. You can also combine one strand of metallic yarn with ordinary stranded yarn to add a little lustre without the weight of a full string of metallic yarn.

Needles

Cross-stitch embroidery is done with blunt tapestry needles. The most common size is a 24 or a 26. A size 24 is used for 6 to 14-count and a size 26 for 16 to 18-count Aida. It is best to use a size 26 needle when you work on even-weave.

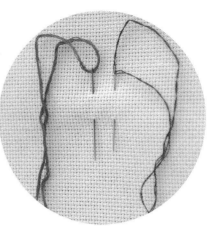

When you are using waste canvas on ordinary fabric, you have to use an embroidery needle with a sharp point so that the needle can be pushed through the fabric without damaging it. When you use beads, it is sometimes necessary to use an ordinary needle to ensure that the needle will fit through the hole in the bead.

Embroidery scissors

A good pair of embroidery scissors is absolutely essential. The scissors must be sharp pointed in order for the yarn to be cut close to the embroidery. This can be an expensive item, but if you look after it properly, you will be able to use it for a lifetime. Keep it away from your family (except if they do embroidery with you) and warn them explicitly that your embroidery scissors may under no circumstances be used for clipping toe nails!

Hoops and frames

Some embroiderers choose not to use a hoop or frame. However, I found that my embroidery is much neater and more even when I use a frame – especially when working with even-weave fabrics.

There are different kinds of frames available. The most popular for cross-stitch embroidery is a ring consisting of two hoops. The hoops are placed underneath and over the embroidery respectively and the screw is tightened until the fabric is firmly stretched.

It is advisable to cover both hoops of the frame with ribbon or masking tape to prevent them from damaging your fabric or embroidery. You can also insert a sheet of tissue paper in the hoop with your embroidery and just tear away the section where you are working. Always loosen the frame overnight or when you will not

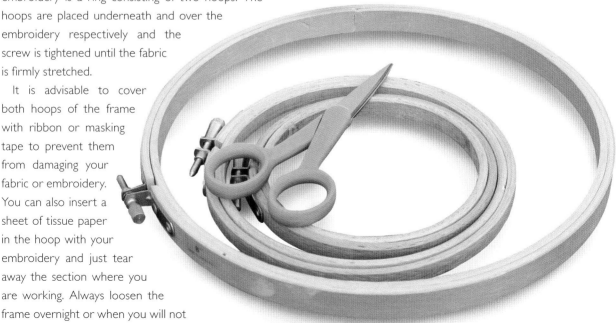

be working for a period of time. That will prevent damage to your embroidery or a mark left by the hoop.

Containers for embroidery yarn

Useful custom-made containers for embroidery yarn are available in different sizes. The amount of yarn you have will determine which size will suit you best. The containers are available from most needlework, embroidery and craft shops. They usually come complete with cardboard or plastic yarn-cards. It is advisable to wind your yarns around these when you store them in the container.

Write the number, as well as the brand name of the yarn on each card so that it will be easy to replace the yarn when you run out. Arrange your yarns in the container according to colours or numbers.

Light and magnifying glass

Using a light with a daylight globe is essential for embroidery, especially when you embroider at night. Light from a daylight globe reduces the strain on your eyes and can be combined with a magnifying glass on an adjustable stand. A smaller magnifying glass is also handy and can make embroidery much easier, especially when you are doing fine work.

Beads and other decorations

Beads combine really well with cross-stitch embroidery and often add a special touch. Buy good quality beads with fairly big holes. I find that Japanese seed beads work really well with embroidery.

Moving eyes are especially popular for children's articles and can be sewn or pasted onto finished items. When you are making small flowers it is sometimes difficult to achieve the rounded shapes. Often it is much easier to use paper or silk flowers. Paper or silk leaves can also be used instead of embroidery.

Miscellaneous

Fabric glue can be used when you want to glue your embroidery onto other fabics. You can also use it to glue beads, flowers or moving eyes to the embroidered fabric. Fabric glue dries clear and has to be left for at least 12 hours to dry properly.

Double-sided tape can be used to stick embroidery onto other materials such as boxes or tins. I also used double-sided tape for the hems on the bookmarks and the pockets of the advent calendar.

Antifray is very useful for embroidery. Apply it to prevent the edges of your work from fraying. It can be used on any article that will not be handled or washed much.

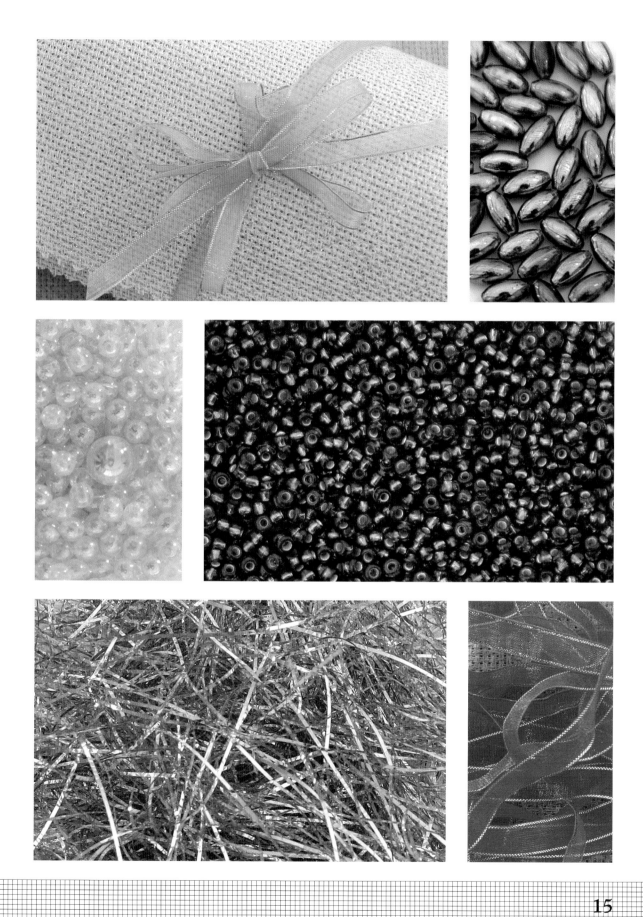

Techniques and hints

Some basic techniques are used for every cross-stitch embroidery project. These are not repeated with the project instructions.

How to read the pattern

Each square on the pattern represents one cross stitch. In some instances quarter stitches have to be worked. They are represented by half a square on the pattern. An asterisk before a colour code indicates that back stitching is worked in that colour.

How to embroider the stitches

The step-by-step photographs on the next page show you exactly how the different stitches are embroidered.

Cross stitch

Cross stitches are formed by two stitches crossing each other diagonally in the centre. All the stitches must lie in the same direction. This means that all the bottom stitches lie in one direction and the top stitches in the opposite direction.

Crosses can be completed one by one, or in horizontal or vertical lines.

For the first stitch, push the needle through from the wrong side to the right side of the fabric in the bottom left corner of the square. Leave a length of yarn of approximately 3 – 5 cm at the back. This will be worked into the stitches at the back afterwards.

Then move the needle one square to the left and one to the top and push from the right side to the wrong side of the fabric. This forms the first half of your stitch.

Bring the needle straight down to the bottom right and push it through from the wrong side of the fabric to the right side of the fabric.

Complete the cross by pushing the needle through to the top left from the right side to the wrong side of the fabric.

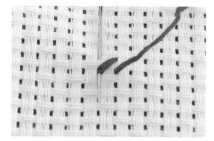

First half of the stitch

Complete the cross

To work a horizontal row of crosses, first complete the entire row in half stitches and then work back to complete the crosses. Make sure that the stitches are all vertical at the back of your work and work away any loose threads in the same direction into the existing stitches.

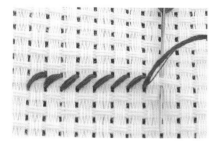

First work the row in half stitches

Work back to complete the crosses

17

Vertical rows can be worked in two ways:

METHOD 1

If you are very concerned about what your work looks like at the back, or if you are entering a competition, you have to use this method. Push the needle through from the wrong side at 1, from front to back at 2, from back to front at 3 and from front

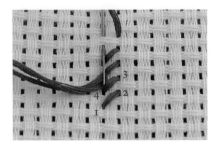

to back at 4. Once you have completed a row of half stitches, you can work back down to complete the crosses.

Using this method the stitches of vertical rows will lie in the same direction on the wrong side of the fabric as with horizontal rows.

Back of fabric

METHOD 2

Using this method the stitches lie horizontally at the back and not vertically as

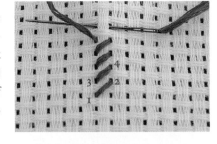

when you work horizontal rows. Many people find this method easier, and there is nothing wrong with it. Push the needle through from back to front at 1, front to back at 2, to the front again at 3, and to the back at 4. Complete a row of half stitches and then work back down to complete the crosses.

Back of fabric

Diagonal rows are usually worked by completing each individual stitch before going on to the next.

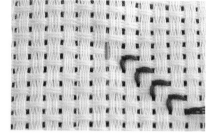

Back of fabric

Cross-stitch embroidery is excellent for the development of children's fine motor skills (see page 92). Let them start with fun, easy motifs, using 6-count Aida and all 6 strands of stranded cotton in bright colours.

Quarter stitches

A quarter stitch is worked by pushing the needle through the centre of the block in which you are working. It does not form a cross.

Half stitches

Half stitches are formed by working only one leg of the cross. It is sometimes used to shade large sections of embroidery (see Four seasons page 31).

Three-quarter stitches

Three-quarter stitches are worked by combining a half stitch and a quarter stitch. Three-quarter stitches are often used when a motif is not outlined with back stitching and neatly finishes off a shaped edge. Three-quarter stitches are not used in any of the patterns in the book.

Back stitching

Most cross-stitch patterns contain back stitching for fine details and to finish and outline motifs. Back stitching is always worked last, unless otherwise indicated, using one less strand than was used for the cross stitches. Back stitch is indicated by a solid line on the pattern.

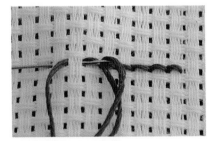 

Beginning and ending off

Never start your embroidery with a knot in the yarn. It forms ugly knobs on the right side and may come loose when the article is washed. If the knot comes loose, the stitches will also come loose and all your hard work will be ruined. Begin and end off your work by neatly weaving the yarn through the existing stitches. When you start, leave a loose end of about 5 cm of yarn and neatly weave it through existing stitches later. Even though nobody sees the wrong side of your work, it is easier to embroider evenly and achieve a professional finish and to avoid mistakes when the wrong side is neat.

A tangle of yarns on the wrong side may cause threads to be pulled through to the right side. The yarn you are using can also become knotted when the wrong side is covered in untidy loose threads that have not been worked away as each section is completed.

Waste canvas

Waste canvas is used for embroidery on fabric without clearly woven squares. use it as follows:

Baste the canvas onto the fabric you want to embroider.

Place the fabric with canvas into an embroidery hoop and embroider the motif according to the pattern

Cut the canvas close to the edge when the embroidery is completed. Pull out the vertical threads first, using a pair of tweezers. The horizontal threads will then be very easy to remove. If you have trouble removing the canvas, you can dampen it a little. Be careful, because too much dampening may result in a sticky mess.

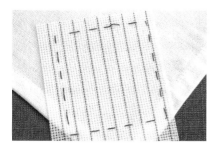

Hints for embroidery

✖ Mark the centre lines of the fabric on which you are working with long basting stitches in a contrasting colour.

✖ Always start your pattern in the centre and make sure that the first stitch is in the right spot.

✖ Always work from the centre outwards so that you can keep any counting to a minimum.

- **✕** If you have to embroider a section of the pattern that is not connected to the rest, you have to count very carefully before starting the new stitches.
- **✕** Embroider the largest sections of single colour first and fill in the detail at a later stage. In this way you advance fairly quickly. It will also be easier to spot any stitches you may have missed.

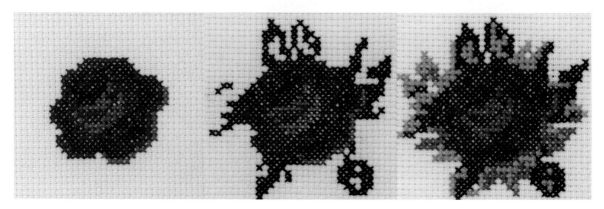

- **✕** Keep the tension of your stitches as even as possible. Pull the yarn fairly tightly, but not so tight that you open the holes in the fabric.
- **✕** Complete all the cross stitches before you do any outlining in back stitch (unless otherwise specified).
- **✕** Don't leave long, loose threads on the wrong side of your embroidery. The threads can easily be caught between other stitches and pulled up to the right side of the work, spoiling it.
- **✕** Enjoy every moment and start your project with the end in sight.

Finishing off your embroidery

Cross-stitch embroidery can be used for a variety of finished items and in the book several suggestions are given.

Embroidery requires concentration and effort. Don't make hard work undone by not finishing off the embroidery properly.

WASHING AND PRESSING

Embroidery can be hand washed. Use a gentle detergent and lukewarm water. If some of the colour happens to run, the article must be rinsed until the water runs clear. However, the quality of embroidery yarns is so good these days that such an occurrence is rare.

Dry the article flat, on a towel, before you press it.

Even if you don't wash the embroidery, you will most probably have to press it, especially if an embroidery frame was used. Place the embroidery right side down on a thick towel and cover with a damp cloth. Press lightly until all creases are re-moved. Never press embroidery on the right side as the stitches will be flattened and it will ruin the texture.

FRAMING

All the patterns in the book are small enough for you to frame the embroidery your-self. However, if you have large projects you would like to be framed, it is advisable to have it done by someone who is experienced in the framing of embroidery.

HINTS FOR FRAMING

- ✗ Use matt glass.
- ✗ Make sure that the embroidery does not warp when you stretch it.
- ✗ Apply double-sided tape as close as possible to the edge of the inner frame where the embroidery is going to show.
- ✗ Gluing batting between the embroidery and the edge of the inner frame creates a very interesting soft, three-dimensional effect.

More hints

× Dampen your yarn slightly to prevent tangling and also to create a good, even finish, especially when you use rayon yarn.

× To save time, thread a few needles with different colours of yarn. Push each needle through a piece of cardboard on which you have written the colour code so that you don't confuse the colours. It saves time because you don't have to thread the needle with a different colour each time you need to change colours.

× There are different ways of **marking the spot** where you are working:

    ××   Mark the place where you have stopped with a pin with a brightly coloured head.

    ××   Mark the spot with a brightly coloured sticker.

    ××   Use a highlighter to mark the completed rows on the pattern – the pattern still has to be visible so that you can find any possible mistakes.

× If you are working with beads you can stick them to a piece of sticky tape to prevent them from rolling around. You can also wrap tape around your finger to facilitate picking up the beads you need for your embroidery.

× Keep metallic yarn in the fridge – it doesn't knot or tangle easily when it is cold.

× It is sometimes difficult to work with metallic yarn, because it consists of very fine filaments that fray easily. It is a good idea to knot the yarn onto the needle. Do it like this: make a loop in the yarn and push the loop through the eye of the needle. Pull the loop over the pointed end of the needle and tighten it at the eye. Gently rub over the eye to knot it into place.

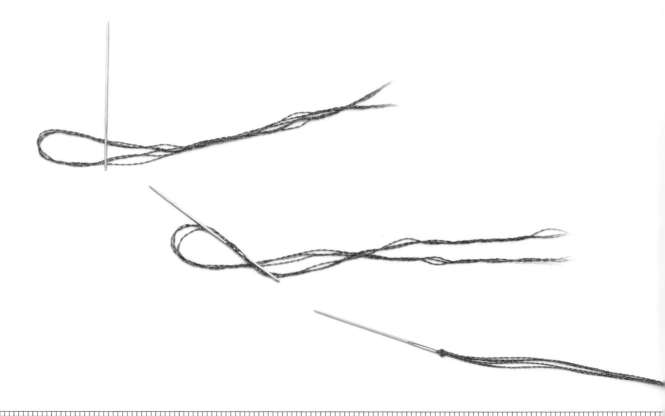

- ✗ Store your embroidery in a white pillow slip when you are not working. It keeps your work clean.
- ✗ Keep a white cloth on your lap when you are working on dark coloured fabrics. The holes in the fabric will then be more visible.
- ✗ If the yarn gets wound up, let the needle hang freely to unwind by itself. Don't continue working with wound up yarn – it stretches and will be thinner than the rest of the yarn and you won't achieve an even finish.
- ✗ To protect your embroidery, tighten a sheet of tissue paper in the embroidery hoop with your fabric, and tear away the paper from sections where you are going to work.

Classic crosses

Classic crosses look beautiful on anything from a bookmark to a Christmas card. Only the outside edge of the cross is embroidered, so you can definitely do it in an evening. I used metallic thread for both crosses, but they look equally stunning worked with ordinary stranded cotton. A cross as bookmark for a teenager's Bible can be done in a bright colour on black. The cross for the card is slightly smaller than that for the bookmark, but you can also use the larger cross for a card.

Personalise the cross by embroidering the date of a special event, for instance confirmation or a christening, onto the vertical beam of the cross.

You will need

25 cm x 15 cm 14-count Aida in white for the bookmark, and corn colour with gold thread for the card
Embroidery yarn as indicated on the pattern
White window card
Double-sided tape
Iron-on interfacing (optional)

Method

1 Embroider the crosses as indicated on the pattern.
2 Use 2 strands of yarn for the cross stitch and 1 for the back stitching.

Making up

BOOKMARK

1 Fold and iron in small hems on three sides of the embroidery and stick them down with double-sided tape.
2 Glue an extra piece of Aida to the back over the hems, or apply iron-on interfacing to the back to cover the hems.
3 Work a row of back stitches along the bottom edge of the bookmark and fray the edge below the stitching.
4 Work gold metallic threads into the frayed edge for a very special effect.

CARD

1 Attach double-sided tape to the inside of the window on the card, as closely as possible to the edge of the window.

2 Press the embroidery down onto the tape and make sure that is is stretched evenly.

More ideas

Embroider the cross on perforated paper or plastic canvas and cut in the shape of a cross. Add a fringe made of metallic thread.

CARD

Grid Size: 33 W x 66 H
Stitches: 30 x 63

DMC	ANCHOR	DESCRIPTION
*E301	-	metallic rust-brown
E168	301	metallic silver

BOOKMARK

Grid Size: 37 W x 73 H
Stitches: 35 x 69

DMC	ANCHOR	DESCRIPTION
*E3852	300	metallic gold
*E168	301	metallic silver

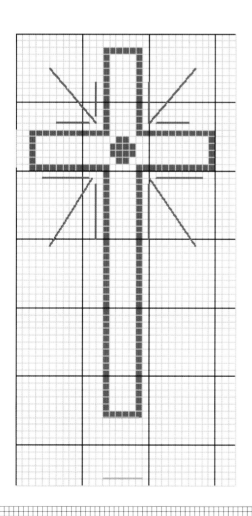

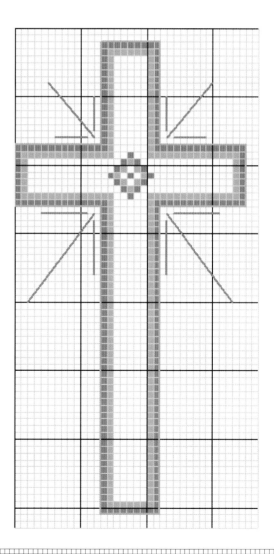

Four seasons

Miniature houses have always intrigued me. These motifs depicting the four seasons can also be framed individually and arranged on a wall, or you can put up only one framed picture according to the season, and replace as the seasons change.

You will need

4 squares (15 cm x 15 cm) light grey 14-count Aida
embroidery yarn as indicated on the pattern
frame with 4 openings, or 4 small frames

Method

1   Embroider the houses as indicated on the pattern.
2   Use 2 strands of yarn for the cross stitch and 1 for the back stitching.

Making up

Because the motifs are small, you can do the framing yourself:
1   Remove the back and glass from a bought frame.
2   Stick double-sided tape close to the edges of the inner frames.
3   Place each motif in the centre of an inner frame and press down firmly.
4   Replace glass and back, and hang it.

More ideas

✗ Embroider one of the houses and glue it onto a window card as a gift for a new-comer in the neighbourhood.
✗ The winter house can be used to make a Christmas card for your friends in the northern hemisphere.

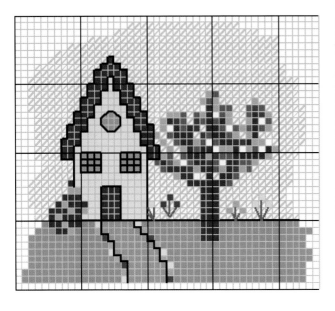

4 SEASONS - SPRING

Grid Size: 46 W x 40 H

Stitches: 44 x 38

DMC	Anchor	Description
*310	403	black
*702	239	kelly green
938	381	coffee brown - ultra dark
703	238	chartreuse
318	399	steel gray - light
Ecru	926	ecru
800	128	delft blue - pale
895	246	hunter green - very dark
604	75	cranberry - light
601	78	cranberry - dark
307	289	lemon
White	2	white

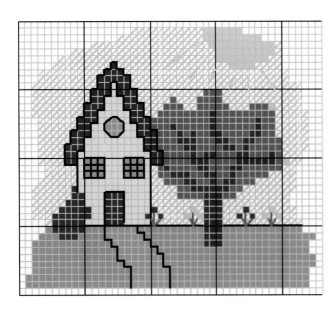

4 SEASONS - SUMMER

Grid Size: 46 W x 40 H

Stitches: 44 x 38

DMC	Anchor	Description
*310	403	black
*702	239	kelly green
938	381	coffee brown - ultra dark
703	238	chartreuse
318	399	steel gray - light
*743	297	yellow - medium
800	128	delft blue - pale
895	246	hunter green - very dark
Ecru	926	ecru
600	59	cranberry - very dark

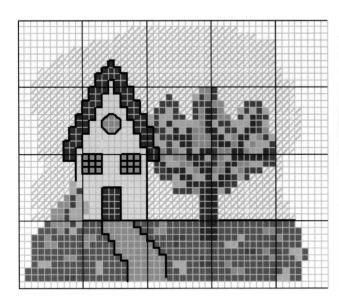

4 SEASONS - AUTUMN

Grid Size: 46 W x 40 H

Stitches: 44 x 38

DMC	Anchor	Description
*310	403	black
938	381	coffee brown - ultra dark
580	267	moss green - dark
318	399	steel gray - light
Ecru	926	ecru
800	128	delft blue - pale
900	333	burnt orange - dark
971	316	pumpkin
742	303	tangerine - light

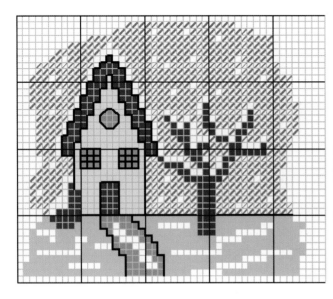

4 SEASONS - WINTER

Grid Size: 46 W x 40 H

Stitches: 44 x 38

DMC	Anchor	Description
*310	403	black
938	381	coffee brown - ultra dk
415	398	pearl grey
318	399	steel gray - light
White	2	white
414	400	steel grey - dark
Ecru	926	ecru

Work the leaves of the tree and the shrub in variegated thread (DMC 51 or Anchor 1305) for a striking autumn effect. In this instance you do the embroidery as a single colour instead of changing colours as indicated on the pattern..

Oriental theme

Black, white and red are strong colours and ideal for teenagers' bedrooms. Most teenagers are fascinated by Oriental themes at one time or another, and the simple, strong lines make this theme very easy to embroider. The theme can be used in different ways in a bedroom. The motifs can be embroidered onto curtains, duvet covers and pillows. The examples shown were all done on white Aida, but can be equally striking on red fabric. Black fabric embroidered with white or red can also be stunning.

The theme needn't be limited to teenagers' bedrooms. It can also create a stunning corner in a living room, dining room or games room.

The motifs are very easy and can be made in no time, as only one colour yarn is used.

You will need

18 cm x 12 cm 14-count Aida for each motif
embroidery yarn as indicated on the pattern
black frames
iron-on interfacing

Method

1   Embroider motifs according to the instructions on the pattern.
2   Use 2 strands of yarn for the cross stitch and 1 for the back stitching.

Making up

1   Cut the motifs to the correct size for the frames and place them into the frames. Make sure that the embroidery is stretched evenly when you place it into the frame.
2   The hanging motif was made up by folding and ironing in narrow hems on all the sides. Apply iron-on interfacing to the back so that it fits neatly over the hems.

More ideas

✗ Outline the motif with back stitching, fray the edges and glue to a plain lamp shade.
✗ Decorate plain white candles in the same fashion.

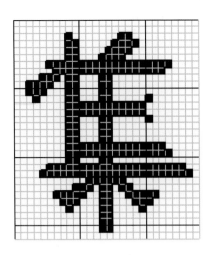

SYMBOL 1

Grid Size: 28 W x 32 H

Stitches: 25 x 29

DMC	ANCHOR	DESCRIPTION
*310	403	black

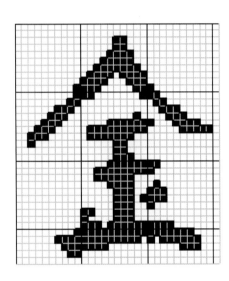

SYMBOL 2

Grid Size: 31 W x 35 H

Stitches: 28 x 32 stitches

DMC	ANCHOR	DESCRIPTION
*310	403	black

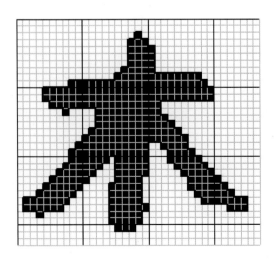

SYMBOL 3

Grid Size: 37 W x 33 H

Stitches: 34 x 29 stitches

DMC	ANCHOR	DESCRIPTION
*310	403	black

Nursery motifs

Most articles made for babies are of necessity small. Therefore small cross-stitch patterns work well on baby clothing and other items. Everything is completed in a jiffy and the itmes are fun to make. The motifs are simple and can be embroidered on any item. The bought bib is made of hemmed Aida, but by using waste canvas (see page 21) you can also embroider on items such as T-shirts and booties. Cheerful, bright colours and soft pastels work equally well for babies.

Embroidery on strips of Aida with a pretty border is ideal for decorating fac cloths, towels and an assortment of containers in the nursery.

You will need

Bib
T-shirt
socks
strips of Aida in different widths
empty containers for miscellaneous items such as cotton wool or cotton buds (I
    used a small Pringles tin)
embroidery yarn as indicated on the pattern
FOR THE BABY PILLOW
4 squares of 15 cm x 15 cm 11-count Aida
5 squares of 15 cm x 15 cm gingham in different colours
soft white cotton for the back of the pillowcase
baby pillow

Method

1 Embroider your chosen motifs according to the patterns.
2 Use waste canvas for the embroidery on the T-shirt
and socks (see page 21).
3 Use 2 strands of yarn for the cross stitch and 1 for
the back stitching, except for the stars for the
baby pillow.
4 Use 3 strands of yarn for the stars for the
baby pillow.

Making up

Carefully remove the waste canvas as described on page 21 after completing the embroidery on the socks and the T-shirt.

BABY PILLOW

1   Alternating the motifs, stitch the embroidered squares to the gingham squares. Make three strips and then stitch the strips together to form a square for the front of the pillowcase.

2   Cut the back large enough to make a fold-over pillow-case and stitch to the front. Finish off the seams neatly, turn inside out and insert the pillow.

FACECLOTH

Top-sew the embroidered strip neatly onto one or two edges of the face cloth.

CONTAINER FOR COTTON WOOL

Make a small hem at each short side of the embroidered strip and join the ends with slip stitch so that the strip fits snugly around the container.

More ideas

✕ Use embroidered strips to decorate baby bed linen or use the strips for curtain tie-backs. You can also use it to decorate the bottom edge of a lamp shade.

✕ Repeat the pattern squares for the pillow on a larger scale to make a pretty duvet cover.

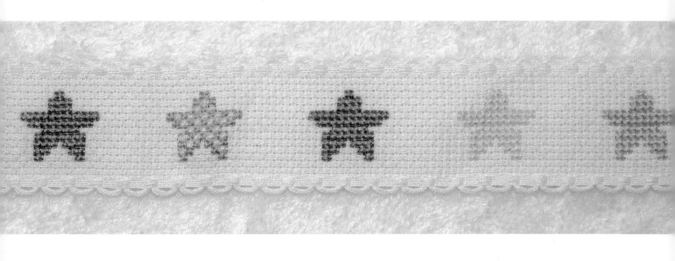

BEAR

Grid Size:	21 W x 23 H	
Stitches:	19 x 21 stitches	

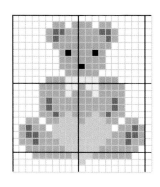

DMC	Anchor	Description
310	403	black
437	362	tan - light
435	369	brown - very light
605	50	cranberry - very light
800	128	delft blue - pale

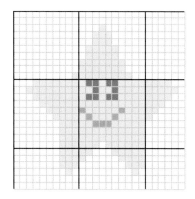

SMILING STAR

Grid Size:	26 W x 26 H	
Stitches:	23 x 22	

DMC	Anchor	Description
996	433	electric blue - medium
604	55	cranberry - light
90	1217	variegated yellow

ROW OF STARS

Grid Size:	97 W x 14 H	
Stitches:	95 x 10	

DMC	Anchor	Description
*605	50	cranberry - very light
*955	206	nile green - light
*745	300	yellow - light pl
*809	130	delft blue
White	2	white

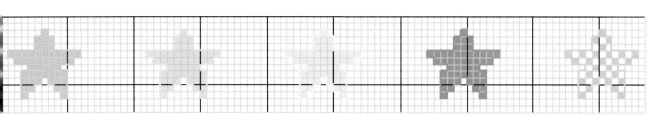

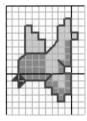

BIRD
Grid Size: 12 W x 16 H
Stitches: 10 x 12

DMC	ANCHOR	DESCRIPTION
606	335	bright orange-red
3755	140	baby blue
3747	120	blue violet - very light
*826	161	blue - medium

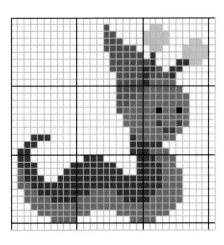

CATERPILLAR
Grid Size: 31 W x 31 H
Stitches: 29 x 29 stitches

DMC	ANCHOR	DESCRIPTION
310	403	black
995	410	electric blue - dark
996	433	electric blue - medium
606	335	bright orange-red
3805	62	cyclamen pink
743	297	yellow - medium

ABC...

These alphabet images are wonderfully versatile and can be used for an assortment of articles. Give your imagination free rein and turn the embroidered images into something special.

Each alphabet block can be framed individually and arranged all over the wall in your toddler's bedroom. Another idea is to make an alphabet book – the ideal gift. This book fits easily into your handbag so you can take it along wherever you go to keep your child occupied.

Plain curtains can be decorated beautifully with the embroidered alphabet blocks. Each alphabet block is worked separately, therefore you never need to carry a large piece of embroidery with you.

It can be lots of fun to embroider these motifs one by one. Before you know it you will have completed the whole alphabet, ready to put the embroidered squares to creative use.

You will need

15 cm x 15 cm 11-count Aida for each letter
embroidery yarn as indicated on every pattern
photo frames in bright colours, curtains or lining, according to your chosen finish
double-sided tape

Method

1   Embroider the motifs as indicated on the pattern.
2   Use 3 strands of yarn for the cross stitch and 2 for the back stitching.

Finish

ALPHABET BOOK

1   Stitch together the consecutive letters in pairs at the top, bottom and outer edges, with right sides together. The edges forming the spine of the book (where the 'pages' come together), are not stitched.
2   Turn the squares inside out and press the seams (iron on a towel and don't iron directly on the embroidery).
3   Stitch all the pages of the book together at the spine with one row of stitching. Finish this edge neatly with bias binding.

FRAMING

1   Cut each square a little larger than the inner frame.
2   Stretch the embroidery evenly over the inner frame, stick down with double-sided tape if needed and fit it into the outer frame.

3   Make interesting arrangements on the wall.

CURTAINS
1   Work a row of back stitching around each motif and fray the edges.
2   Decide where you want to place the motifs on the curtain and baste them onto the curtain with small basting stitches. It is advisable to pin the motifs to the curtain first until you are satisfied with the arrangement. Stitch into place just inside the row of back stitching.

More ideas

✖ Stitch together 6 alphabet squares and use it as cover for a foam rubber cube of the same size to make soft building blocks for a baby.

✖ Embroider your child's name or initials and attach to his bedroom door.

✖ Embroider some of the motifs without the letters onto a bib or towel. For example, the fairy would look really pretty on a curtain tie-back – and how about a row of whales as a border pattern for a curtain?

ALPHABET A

Grid Size: 36 W x 36 H
Stitches: 34 x 34

DMC	Anchor	Description
*310	403	black
702	239	kelly green
580	267	moss green - dark
700	229	christmas green - bright
White	2	white
321	47	christmas red
498	20	christmas red - dark

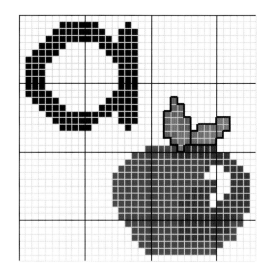

ALPHABET B

Grid Size: 41 W x 37 H
Stitches: 39 x 35

DMC	Anchor	Description
600	59	cranberry - very dark
726	295	topaz - light
553	98	violet
608	333	bright orange
333	119	blue violet - very dark
943	188	aquamarine - medium
910	228	emerald green - dark
995	410	electric blue - dark
*310	403	black

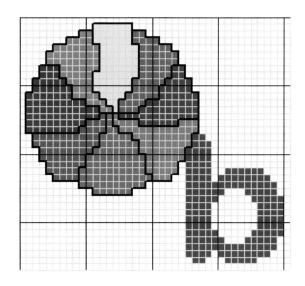

ALPHABET C

Grid Size: 37 W x 33 H
Stitches: 35 x 31

DMC	Anchor	Description
*310	403	black
606	335	bright orange-red
745	300	yellow - light pale
307	289	lemon
701	227	christmas green - light

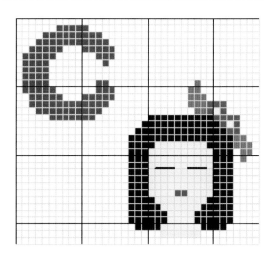

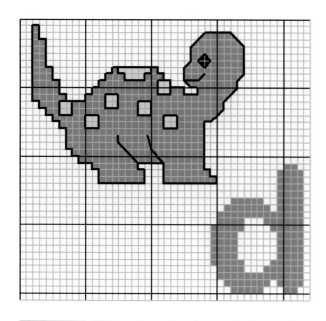

ALPHABET D

Grid Size: 44 W x 41 H
Stitches: 41 x 39

DMC	Anchor	Description
*310	403	black
703	238	chartreuse
307	289	lemon

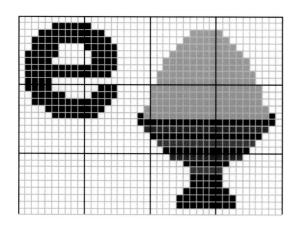

ALPHABET E

Grid Size: 40 W x 29 H
Stitches: 38 x 27

DMC	Anchor	Description
700	228	christmas green - bright
606	335	bright orange-red
437	362	tan - light

ALPHABET F

Grid Size: 43 W x 40 H
Stitches: 41 x 37

DMC	Anchor	Description
600	59	cranberry - very dark
White	2	white
605	50	cranberry - very light
*E168	301	metallic silver
951	366	tawny - light
437	362	tan - light
*310	403	black

ALPHABET G

Grid Size:	41 W x 41 H	
Stitches:	38 x 38	

DMC	Anchor	Description
310	403	black
605	50	cranberry - very light
743	297	yellow - medium
White	2	white
604	75	cranberry - light
*318	399	steel grey - light

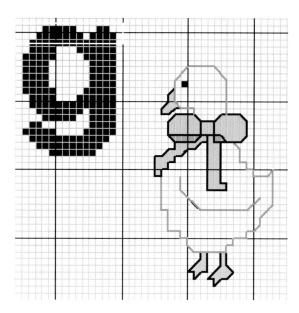

Using fabric glue, stick down paper flowers in the garden instead of working them in cross stitch.

ALPHABET H

Grid Size:	50 W x 50 H	
Stitches:	41 x 38	

DMC	Anchor	Description
824	164	blue - very dark
702	239	kelly green
318	399	steel gray - light
*317	400	pewter gray
321	47	christmas red
828	158	blue - very light
White	2	white
307	289	lemon

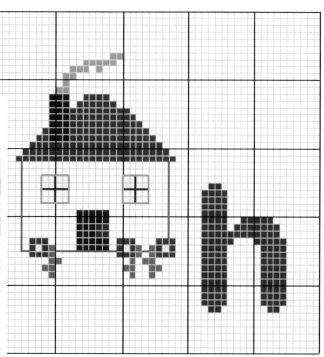

Replace the apple's cross-stitched leaves with silk leaves attached to the ends at the base of the leaves, as indicated on the pattern. Alternatively stick them down with fabric glue.

Thanks to the scrapbooking craze, paper flowers are widely available in craft and stationery shops. Use them (with fabric glue) in the Chinese girl's hair instead of embroidering flowers.

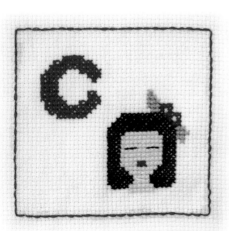

ALPHABET I

Grid Size: 40 W x 37 H
Stitches: 37 x 34

DMC	Anchor	Description
White	2	white
3755	140	baby blue
*317	400	pewter grey
318	399	steel grey - light
415	398	pearl grey

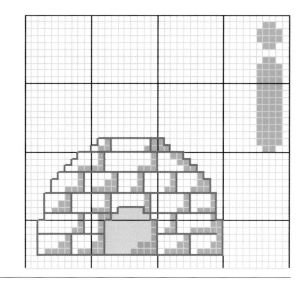

ALPHABET J

Grid Size: 47 W x 36 H
Stitches: 44 x 34

DMC	Anchor	Description
435	369	brown - very light
726	295	topaz -light
*740	316	tangerine
972	298	canary - deep
*310	403	black

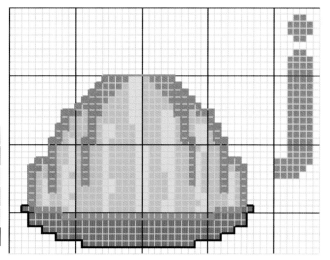

ALPHABET K

Grid Size: 48 W x 45 H
Stitches: 45 x 42

DMC	Anchor	Description
*310	403	black
820	134	royal blue - very dark
300	352	mahogany - very dark
666	46	christmas red - bright
*E3852	300	metallic gold
Ecru	926	ecru

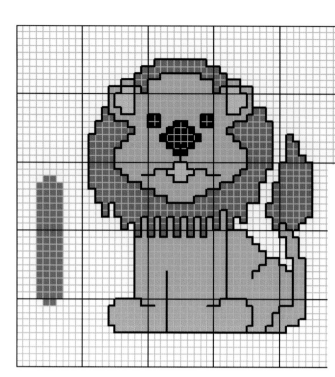

ALPHABET L

Grid Size: 50 W x 50 H
Stitches: 42 x 40

DMC	Anchor	Description
*310	403	black
972	298	canary - deep
3826	1049	golden brown
353	8	peach

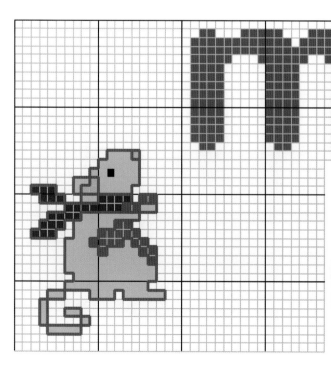

ALPHABET M

Grid Size: 43 W x 44 H
Stitches: 40 x 42

DMC	Anchor	Description
415	398	pearl grey
600	59	cranberry - very dark
776	24	pink - medium
*317	400	pewter grey
310	403	black

*After completing the tree, work the eggs in
back stitch. The nest is worked afterwards by
randomly stitching long and short stitches in
the colours indicated.*

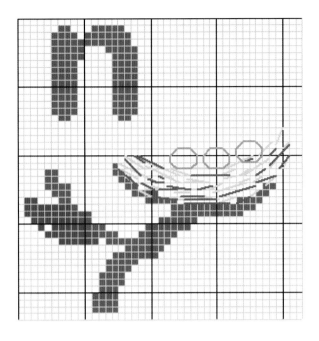

ALPHABET N

Grid Size: 43 W x 44 H
Cloth Count: 14
Stitches: 40 x 42

DMC	Anchor	Description
*318	399	steel gray - light
700	229	christmas green - bright
*743	297	yellow - medium
White	2	white
*301	349	mahogany - medium

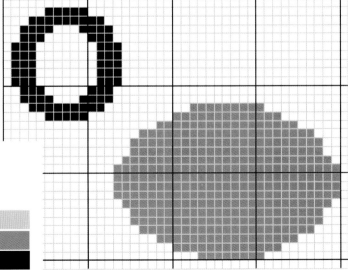

ALPHABET O

Grid Size: 41 W x 31 H
Stitches: 39 x 29

DMC	Anchor	Description
740	316	tangerine
310	403	black

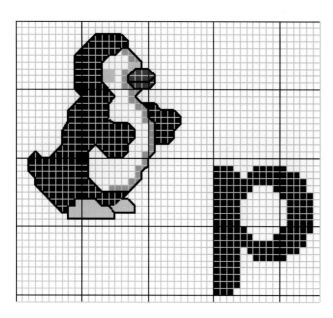

ALPHABET P

Grid Size: 46 W x 41 H

Stitches: 43 x 38

DMC	Anchor	Description
*310	403	black
318	399	steel gray - light
606	335	bright orange-red
743	297	yellow - medium
White	2	white
605	50	cranberry - very light

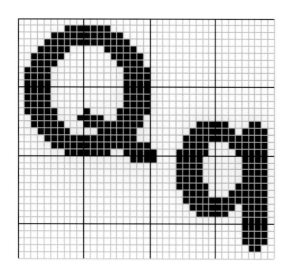

ALPHABET Q

Grid Size: 39 W x 35 H

Stitches: 37 x 33

DMC	Anchor	Description
820	134	royal blue - very dark

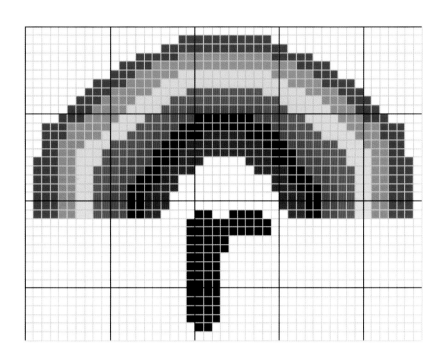

ALPHABET R

Grid Size: 47 W x 36 H

Stitches: 45 x 34

DMC	Anchor	Description
550	102	violet - very dark
820	134	royal blue - very dark
995	410	electric blue - dark
701	227	christmas green - light
726	295	topaz - light
740	316	tangerine
666	46	christmas red - bright
310	403	black

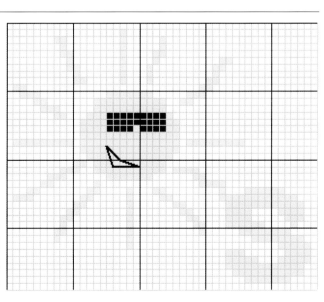

ALPHABET S

Grid Size: 45 W x 31 H

Stitches: 43 x 28

DMC	Anchor	Description
*973	290	canary - bright
310	403	black

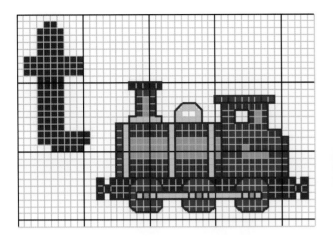

ALPHABET T

Grid Size: 45 W x 31 H
Stitches: 43 x 28

DMC	Anchor	Description
White	2	white
699	923	christmas green
471	266	avocado green - very light
666	46	christmas red - bright
*938	381	coffee brown - ultra dark
726	295	topaz - light

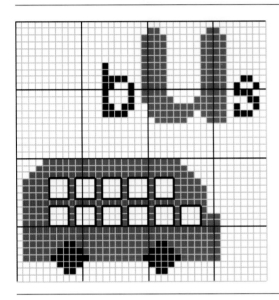

ALPHABET U

Grid Size: 38 W x 38 H
Stitches: 36 x 36

DMC	Anchor	Description
*310	403	black
700	229	christmas green - bright
606	335	bright orange-red
White	2	white

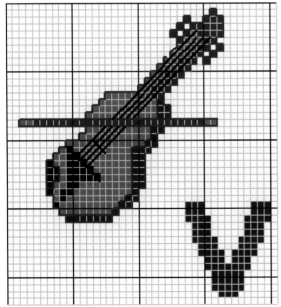

Work the violen strings in back stitch before working the bow in cross stitch and back stitching.

ALPHABET V

Grid Size: 41 W x 44 H
Stitches: 38 x 42

DMC	Anchor	Description
*310	403	black
838	380	beige brown - very dark
300	352	mahogany - very dark
301	349	mahogany - medium

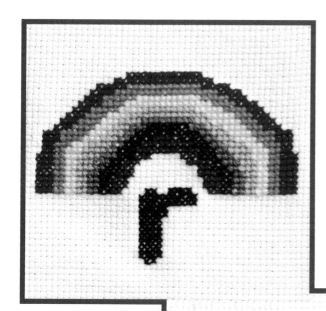

Make a magic wand for the fairy by dipping a toothpick in silver craft paint, allow to dry and attach a glued star to both sides at the top. Attach to the embroidery by threading through the existing stitches.

Use a moving eye for the whale instead of cross stitches in the position indicated on the pattern. Attach with fabric glue.

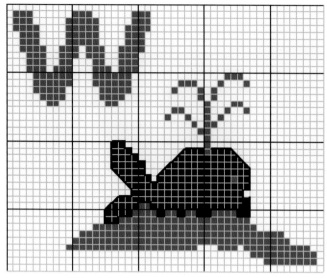

ALPHABET W

Grid Size: 48 W x 39 H
Stitches: 46 x 37

DMC	ANCHOR	DESCRIPTION
*310	403	black
995	410	electric blue - dark

Dolly up the whale even more by embroidering its water spout in beads rather than cross stitches.

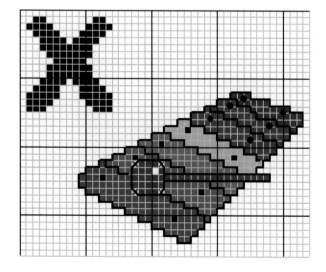

ALPHABET X

Grid Size: 44 W x 36 H
Stitches: 42 x 33

DMC	ANCHOR	DESCRIPTION
*310	403	black
995	410	electric blue - dark
553	98	violet
943	188	aquamarine - medium
972	298	canary - deep
606	335	bright orange-red
699	923	christmas green
321	47	christmas red
666	46	christmas red - bright
433	371	brown - medium
White	2	white

ALPHABET Y

Grid Size: 39 W x 35 H

Stitches: 37 x 32

DMC	Anchor	Description
702	239	kelly green
*561	212	jade - very dark
550	102	violet - very dark
700	700	christmas green - bright
White	2	white
327	101	violet - dark
553	98	violet

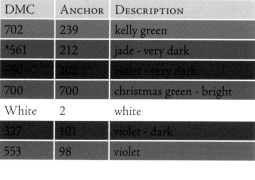

For an interesting three-dimensional effect, use white seed-beads instead of white cross stitches.

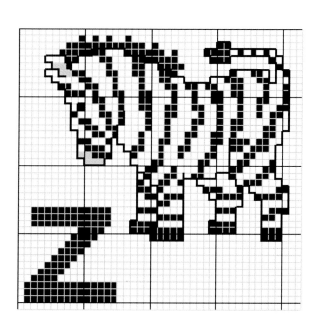

ALPHABET Z

Grid Size: 43 W x 41 H

Stitches: 40 x 39

DMC	Anchor	Description
*310	403	black
605	50	cranberry - very light
White	2	white

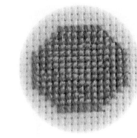

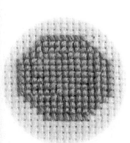

Cool teen motifs

Teenagers are very fussy and will not readily accept something hand made that they don't regard as funky or cool. I decorated two bought cushions for my teenagers with cross stitch and beads, and their friends are crazy about them. The embroidery was glued onto the cushions with fabric glue and now they both have a unique cushion that cannot be bought in any shop.

The funky motif on the green cushion will most probably not be completed in one sitting, but the end result makes the time spent well worthwhile. The hearts in polka dots on the pink cushion are incredibly easy to make and the simple embroidered flowers on the lamp shade were done in a jiffy. The note card is made from plastic canvas and your teenager can write or stick any message onto it.

POLKA-DOT CUSHION

You will need

covered cushion
20 cm x 20 cm 18-count Aida in soft pink
embroidery yarn as indicated on the pattern
fabric glue
Antifray
flower beads

Method

1 Place the Aida into an embroidery hoop.
2 Embroder polka-dot hearts randomly on the Aida. Decide beforehand where you want to start each motif.
3 Use 2 strands of yarn for the cross stitch

Making up

1 Cut the Aida to the correct size and apply Antifray before glueing it to the cushion with fabric glue.
2 String flower beads and attach the string with fabric glue to finish off the embroidery.

STAR CUSHION

You will need

20 cm x 20 cm 18-count Aida in a soft pink
embroidery yarn as indicated on the pattern
fabric glue
green beads

Method

1 Embroider the funky motif as indicated on the pattern.
2 Use 2 strands of yarn for the cross stitch and 1 for the back stitching.

Making up

1 Fold hems in all sides and press (do not iron over the embroidery).
2 Glue the embroidery to the cushion with fabric glue.
3 String beads and glue in place with fabric glue to finish the embroidery.

LAMPSHADE

You will need

2 x 8 cm x 8 cm squares of 18-count Aida in a soft pink
embroidery yarn as indicated on the pattern
2 flat beads for the flower centres
lampshade
fabric glue

Method

1   Embroider flowers as indicated on the pattern, leaving the centres where the
beads will be glued.
2   Use 2 strands of yarn for the cross stitch and 1 for the back stitching.

Making up

1   Frame the flowers in back stitching and fray the outer edges.
2   Glue the embroidery onto the lampshade with fabric glue.
3   Glue a flat bead in the middle of each flower.

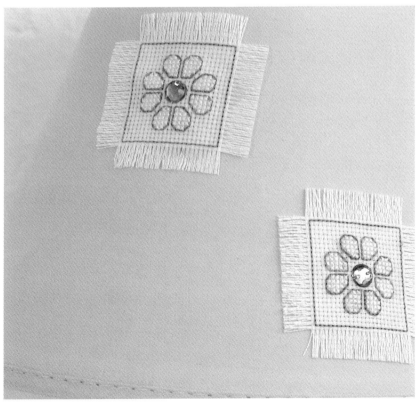

NOTE CARD

You will need

10 cm x 7 cm plastic canvas
embroidery yarn as indicated on the pattern

Method

1 Embroider the motif as indicated on the pattern.
2 Use 2 strands of yarn for the cross stitch.
3 Neatly cut the plastic canvas away around the edge of the embroidery. Work with care, stopping one row away from the embroidery so that the stitches don't come loose.

More ideas

✕ Embroider the flowers onto a pillow case.
✕ Decorate a notebook or jewellery case with the embroidered flowers.
✕ Use plastic canvas with an embroidered frame as a photo frame for scrapbooking, or embroider words onto the plastic canvas for uniquel captions for photographs.
✕ Embroider the motif for the star cushion onto a finished Aida strip and use it as a bookmark.

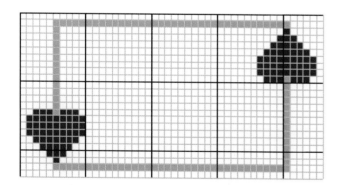

CARD

Grid Size: 46 W x 24 H
Stitches: 44 x 22

DMC	Anchor	Description
604	75	cranberry - light
333	119	blue violet - very dark

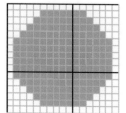

POLKA-DOT HEART

Grid Size: 17 W x 16 H
Stitches: 15 x 14

DMC	Anchor	Description
907	255	parrot green - light
604	75	cranberry - light

FLOWER

Grid Size:	19 W x 19 H	
Stitches:	7 x 17	

DMC	Anchor	Description
White	2	white
211	108	lavender – light
604	75	cranberry - light

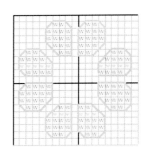

GIRL

Grid Size:	47 W x 95 H	
Stitches:	45 x 93	

DMC	Anchor	Description
310	403	black
743	297	yellow - medium
353	8	peach
553	89	violet
5283	301	metallic silver
307	289	lemon
907	255	parrot green - light

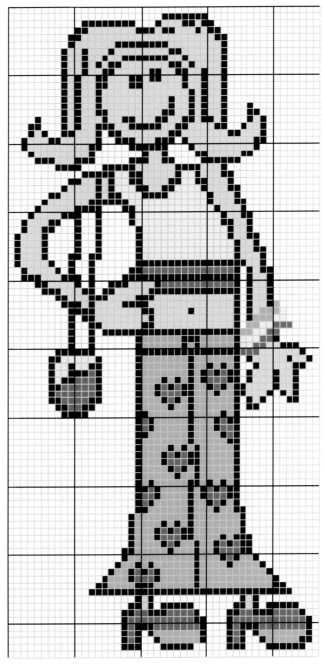

Fun spirals

This simple spiral pattern can really be completed in a wink! Work a few in a row in neon colours on black for an eye-catching bookmark, or just one on a square to decorate a small box for an interesting gift. Only one spiral with a pretty frame is needed for the pencil holder. All these items are ideal gifts for teenagers, but if you use more subdued colours it could work for anybody. Black spirals on white fabric look very elegant.

You will need

20 cm x 10 cm 14-count black Aida each for the bookmark and pencil holder and 6cm x 6cm for the box
small tin for pens (the small size Pringles container works well)
brightly coloured box
double-sided tape
black iron-on interfacing

Method

1 Work the spirals as indicated on the pattern. The pattern for the bookmark is complete.
2 Work only one spiral on the Aida for the pencil holder, and one on the square for the box.
3 Use 2 strands of yarn for the cross stitch and 1 for the back stitching.

Making up

BOOKMARK
1 Work a row of back stitching at the bottom edge and fray the lower edge.
2 Fold and press down small hems on the other three sides of the bookmark and stick down with double-sided tape. Glue an extra piece of Aida to the back over the hems, or reinforce the back with iron-on interfacing over the hemmed edges

PENCIL HOLDER
1 Glue the embroidery to the tin with double-sided tape.
2 Neatly fold over the top end bottom edges and glue down securely to ensure that the tin is finished neatly.

BOX

1 Make back stitches around the design and fray the edges.
2 Glue onto the box with double-sided tape

More ideas

Decorate a diary with a number of spirals embroidered on individual squares. Make them individually, work in squares around the design with back stitches, fray the edges and glue them onto a bought diary.

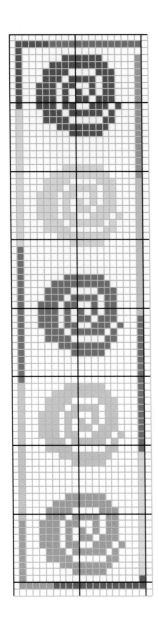

SPIRALS

Grid Size: 21 W x 82 H

Stitches: 19 x 80

DMC	ANCHOR	DESCRIPTION
602	63	cranberry - medium
307	289	lemon
907	255	parrot green
970	316	pumpkin - light
996	433	electric blue - medium

*If you wish to work in neon colours, as I have done here,
use DMC's E980 (yellow) and E990 (green) instead of the
normal bright yellow and green specified in the pattern.*

Romantic roses

Initially I wanted to embroider the roses onto very fine even-weave to compliment the sheer duvet cover, but the contrast between the 11-count Aida and the sheer bed linen was so enchanting that I decided to use the Aida. This beautiful duvet cover and matching cushion transform the bedroom into something really special. The embroidered motifs can be finished easily and in no time at all and before you know it you will have enough motifs to complete the project. You can use more or fewer motifs – the choice is yours. The motifs can also be worked in other colours to suit your specific colour scheme.

You will need

18 cm x 18 cm 11-count Aida for each rose
embroidery yarn as indicated on the pattern
antique-look frame

Method

1   Stitch the rose motif according to the pattern.
2   Use 3 strands for the cross stitch.

Making up

1 Fold and press down small hems all round.
2 Attach the motifs to the cushion or duvet cover with neat slip stitches.
3 For a rose in a frame, cut the embroidery to the correct size and place into the frame.

More ideas

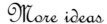

× Embroider extra motifs to attach to a lamp shade.
× Use waste canvas and embroider the pattern directly onto a sheet, table runner or pillowcase.
× Repeat the design on a hand towel.

ROSE

Grid Size: 35 W x 33 H
Stitches: 33 x 31

DMC	Anchor	Description
814	45	garnet - dark
321	47	christmas red
666	46	christmas red - bright
892	33	carnation - medium
987	244	forest green - dark
989	242	forest green
890	218	pistachio green - ultra dark

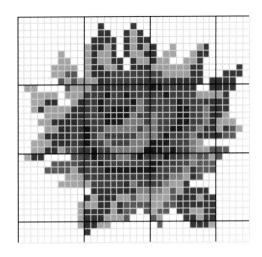

Stylish napery

Even-weave fabrics are hard wearing and ideal to use for table linen. Napkins and placemats can be transformed into something special by embroidering a small motif on each. Unfortunately embroidery fabrics are very expensive so if you want to save money you should buy plain napkins and table runners and embroider the motifs onto them using waste canvas.

Custom-made tablecloths and napkins can be bought at most embroidery shops. These are made from fine linen with a strip of Aida, on which you can embroider, woven into the cloth.

Ivy leaves are a classic motif and will always be a good choice. You can also embellish table linen with embroidered Christmas motifs to use during the festive season.

You will need

custom-made placemat or 50 cm x 35 cm even-weave for each placemat
embroidery yarn as indicated on the pattern
small strip of finished Aida for napkin ring

Method

1   Embroider the ivy motif in the corner of the placemat as shown on the pattern.
2   Use 2 strands of yarn for the cross stitch and 1 for the back stitching.
3   Embroider the motif for the napkin ring on the strip of Aida.
4   Using slip stitch, neatly join the short ends to form a ring.

More ideas

✗ Embroider the ivy design on the corner of a napkin.
✗ Make less formal table linen by embroidering spirals (see page 70) in bright colours as a border pattern for placemats. Use Aida rather than even-weave.
✗ Embroider the ivy design on a tray cloth as a gift for a special friend.
✗ You can also use the ivy design for the cover of a recipe book.

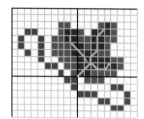

NAPKIN RING

Grid Size: 19 W x 16 H
Stitches: 17 x 13

DMC	Anchor	Description
433	358	brown - medium
3346	257	hunter green
890	879	pistachio green - ultra dark
*3348	265	yellow green - light

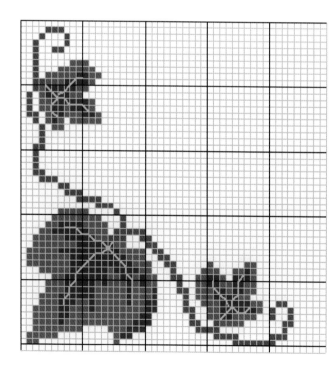

PLACEMAT

Grid Size: 49 W x 51 H
Stitches: 43 x 49

DMC	Anchor	Description
3346	257	hunter green
890	879	pistachio green - ultra dark
433	371	brown - medium
*3348	265	yellow green - light

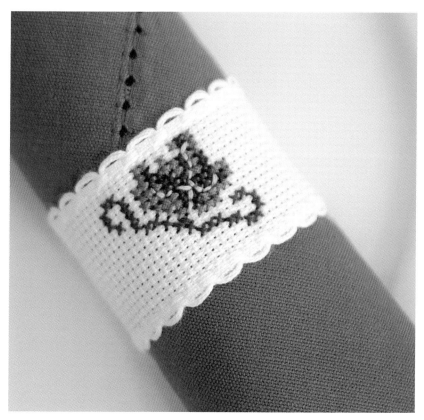

Monograms

In the Victorian age, the alphabet was the main theme of virutally all samplers. The 26 letters of the alphabet were embroidered on fabric and to that messages, slogans and sayings were added. Monograms are a remnant from these practices.

Monograms are always a very popular choice if you want to give a personalised gift. There is an old adage stating that unless you have given of your time, you haven't really given anything. Giving someone something with an embroidered initial on it, indicates that it was made specially for that person and not bought in haste.

The letters can be embroidered on napkins for a special occasion, or on facecloths for every day use. Emboider your family's initials on napkins so that everyone knows which one belongs to him or her.

The letters I have used can all be decorated with beads. The beading pattern stays the same throughout – just use them in different places on the letters. You needn't use them where they appear on the pattern – just put them on wherever you like. Use your own initiative and move them around until you are satisfied with the design.

The monogram on the broach was worked on 22-count even-weave with one strand of yarn. The 'A' was embroidered on 14-count Aida and the 'S' with 14-count waste canvas on a plain napkin.

You will need

embroidery fabic of your choice
embroidery yarn as indicated on the pattern

Method

1   Work the motif according to the instructions on the pattern.
2   Use as many strands of yarn as required by the fabric you are working on.
3   Make up according to the item you are making.

More ideas

✘ You needn't use beads. Cross stitches can be made, or even paper flowers can be glued down. Paper and silk flowers are very fashionable these days.
✘ Experiment with different colours. Contrasting colours have a totally different effect from monotones. Monotones, for instance white on white or cream on cream, result in a very sophisticated look.

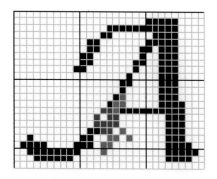

MONOGRAM A

Grid Size: 29 W x 23 H

Stitches: 27 x 21

DMC	ANCHOR	DESCRIPTION
310	403	black
702	239	kelly green
606	335	bright orange-red

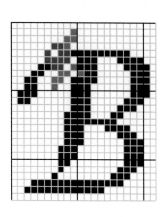

MONOGRAM B

Grid Size: 22 W x 26 H

Stitches: 20 x 24

DMC	ANCHOR	DESCRIPTION
310	403	black
702	239	kelly green
606	335	bright orange-red

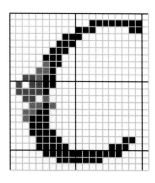

MONOGRAM C

Grid Size: 21 W x 23 H

Stitches: 19 x 21

DMC	ANCHOR	DESCRIPTION
310	403	black
702	239	kelly green
606	335	bright orange-red

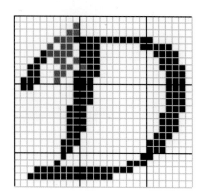

MONOGRAM D

Grid Size: 27 W x 25 H

Stitches: 25 x 23

DMC	ANCHOR	DESCRIPTION
310	403	black
702	239	kelly green
606	335	bright orange-red

MONOGRAM E

Grid Size: 20 W x 23 H
Stitches: 18 x 21

DMC	ANCHOR	DESCRIPTION
310	403	black
702	239	kelly green
606	335	bright orange-red

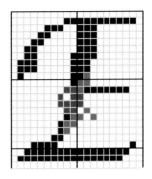

MONOGRAM F

Grid Size: 24 W x 32 H
Stitches: 22 x 30

DMC	ANCHOR	DESCRIPTION
310	403	black
702	239	kelly green
606	335	bright orange-red

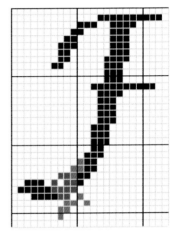

MONOGRAM G

Grid Size: 21 W x 30 H
Stitches: 19 x 28

DMC	ANCHOR	DESCRIPTION
310	403	black
702	239	kelly green
606	335	bright orange-red

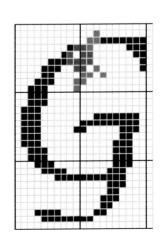

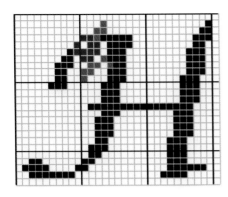

MONOGRAM H

Grid Size: 31 W x 25 H
Stitches: 29 x 23

DMC	Anchor	Description
310	403	black
702	239	kelly green
606	335	bright orange-red

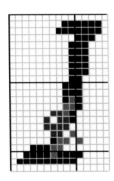

MONOGRAM I

Grid Size: 15 W x 23 H
Stitches: 13 x 21

DMC	Anchor	Description
310	403	black
702	239	kelly green
606	335	bright orange-red

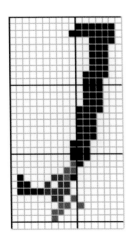

MONOGRAM J

Grid Size: 17 W x 31 H
Stitches: 15 x 29

DMC	Anchor	Description
310	403	black
702	239	kelly green
606	335	bright orange-red

MONOGRAM K

Grid Size: 30 W x 24 H
Stitches: 28 x 22

DMC	Anchor	Description
310	403	black
702	239	kelly green
606	335	bright orange-red

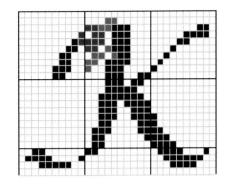

MONOGRAM L

Grid Size: 21 W x 25 H
Stitches: 19 x 23

DMC	Anchor	Description
310	403	black
702	239	kelly green
606	335	bright orange-red

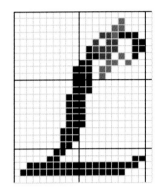

MONOGRAM M

Grid Size: 34 W x 23 H
Stitches: 32 x 21

DMC	Anchor	Description
310	403	black
702	239	kelly green
606	335	bright orange-red

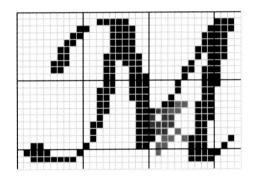

MONOGRAM N

Grid Size: 35 W x 27 H
Stitches: 33 x 25

DMC	Anchor	Description
310	403	black
702	239	kelly green
606	335	bright orange-red

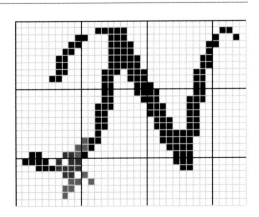

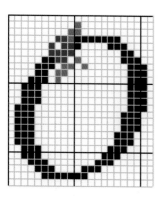

MONOGRAM O

Grid Size: 22 W x 25 H
Stitches: 20 x 23

DMC	ANCHOR	DESCRIPTION
310	403	black
702	239	kelly green
606	335	bright orange-red

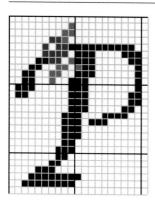

MONOGRAM P

Grid Size: 21 W x 26 H
Stitches: 19 x 24

DMC	ANCHOR	DESCRIPTION
310	403	black
702	239	kelly green
606	335	bright orange-red

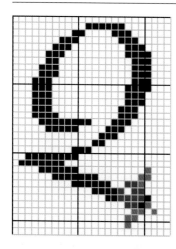

MONOGRAM Q

Grid Size: 24 W x 32 H
Stitches: 21 x 30

DMC	ANCHOR	DESCRIPTION
310	403	black
702	239	kelly green
606	335	bright orange-red

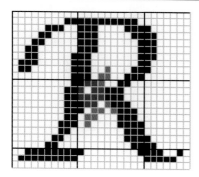

MONOGRAM R

Grid Size: 27 W x 23 H
Stitches: 25 x 21

DMC	ANCHOR	DESCRIPTION
310	403	black
702	239	kelly green
606	335	bright orange-red

MONOGRAM S

Grid Size: 17 W x 26 H

Stitches: 15 x 24

DMC	Anchor	Description
310	403	black
702	239	kelly green
606	335	bright orange-red

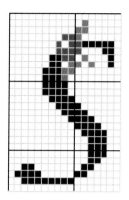

MONOGRAM T

Grid Size: 25 W x 25 H

Stitches: 23 x 23

DMC	Anchor	Description
310	403	black
702	239	kelly green
606	335	bright orange-red

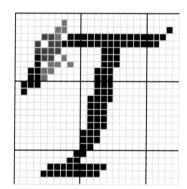

MONOGRAM U

Grid Size: 28 W x 26 H

Stitches: 26 x 24

DMC	Anchor	Description
310	403	black
702	239	kelly green
606	335	bright orange-red

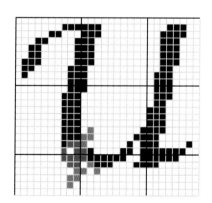

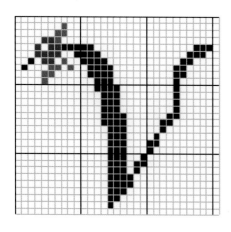

MONOGRAM V

Grid Size: 31 W x 29 H
Stitches: 29 x 27

DMC	Anchor	Description
310	403	black
702	239	kelly green
606	335	bright orange-red

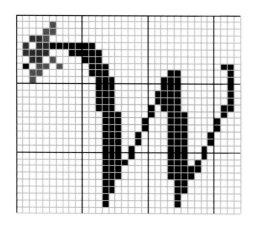

MONOGRAM W

Grid Size: 34 W x 29 H
Stitches: 32 x 27

DMC	Anchor	Description
310	403	black
702	239	kelly green
606	335	bright orange-red

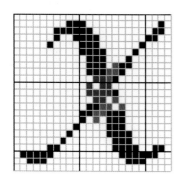

MONOGRAM X

Grid Size: 24 W x 23 H
Stitches: 22 x 21

DMC	Anchor	Description
310	403	black
702	239	kelly green
606	335	bright orange-red

MONOGRAM Y ALT

Grid Size: 22 W x 32 H
Stitches: 20 x 30

DMC	Anchor	Description
702	239	kelly green
600	59	cranberry - very dark
602	77	cranberry - medium
211	108	lavender - light

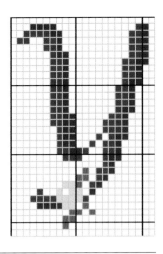

MONOGRAM Y

Grid Size: 22 W x 32 H
Stitches: 20 x 30

DMC	Anchor	Description
310	403	black
702	239	kelly green
606	335	bright orange-red

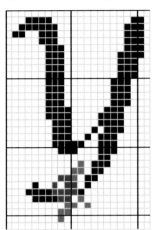

MONOGRAM Z ALT

Grid Size: 20 W x 25 H
Stitches: 18 x 23

DMC	Anchor	Description
702	239	kelly green
208	110	lavender - very dark
209	105	lavender - dark
550	102	violet - very dark

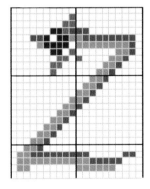

MONOGRAM Z

Grid Size: 20 W x 25 H
Stitches: 18 x 23

DMC	Anchor	Description
310	403	black
702	239	kelly green
606	335	bright orange-red

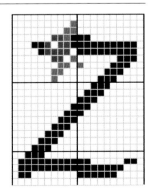

Fruit for jam

Any jar of home-made or bought jam can be made extra special by embroidering a cover for the lid. All these simple patterns can be embroidered in one sitting. Choose your pattern according to the kind of jam in the jar.

A honey jar can also be rounded off beautifully with the motif of a honey comb and bees.

The embroidered fruit motifs also look stunning in a small frame.

The edges of the embroidery can be finished off in different ways. You can work a row of back stitching around the motif and fray the edges, or you can frame the motif by working a design, as with the honey-comb motif. You can also decorate the edge with a piece of lace, or simply apply antifray to prevent fraying.

Simply cut a circle around the embroidered fruits, apply antifray and glue to the lid with fabric glue. Then you don't have to take off the cover every time you open the jar.

You will need
10 cm x 10 cm 16-count Aida for each fruit
10 cm x 10 cm 14-count Aida for the honey motif
embroidery yarn as indicated on the pattern
25 cm matching fine ribbon for the covers
antifray
fabric glue

Method
1 Embroider each motif as indicated on the pattern.
2 Use 2 strands of yarn for the cross stitch and 1 for the back stitch.

Making up
Make up as desired or as described in the introduction and tie the covers over the lids of the jam jars with stranded cotton or fine ribbon.

More ideas

- ✘ Embroider a row of fruit on the edge of a dish cloth or tray cloth, or a single fruit onto the corner of a napkin.
- ✘ The fruits can also be embroidered on a finished Aida strip to decorate shelves in the kitchen. If you have a cupboard with glass doors in your kitchen, such a strip on the front of the shelves will look rather striking.

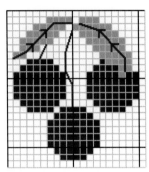

CHERRIES

Grid Size: 21 W x 23 H
Stitches: 19 x 21

DMC	Anchor	Description
471	266	avocado green - very light

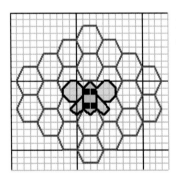

HONEYCOMB

Grid Size: 24 W x 23 H
Stitches: 22 x 20

DMC	Anchor	Description
*301	349	mahogany - medium
726	295	topaz - light
310	403	black
800	128	delft blue - pale

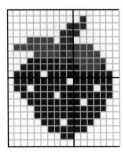

STRAWBERRIES

Grid Size: 17 W x 20 H
Stitches: 15 x 18

DMC	Anchor	Description
702	239	kelly green
700	229	christmas green - bright
666	46	christmas red - bright

ORANGE

Grid Size:	25 W x 24 H	
Stitches:	22 x 21	

DMC	Anchor	Description
740	316	tangerine
742	303	tangerine - light
745	300	yellow - light pale
*301	349	mahogany - medium

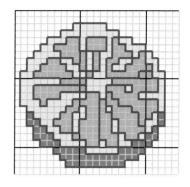

PINEAPPLE

Grid Size:	24 W x 34 H	
Stitches:	22 x 30	

DMC	ANCHOR	DESCRIPTION
700	229	christmas green - bright
726	295	topaz - light
972	298	canary - deep
*301	349	mahogany - medium

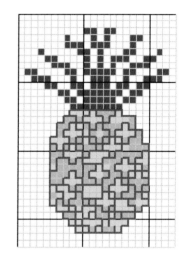

Busy little fingers

Cross-stitch embroidery is excellent for developing fine motor skills in children and improving their concentration. Let them use 6- and 8-count Aida. The squares are big and counting them is not too difficult. Don't separate the yarn as all 6 strands can be used on this size Aida.

The patterns are really very easy to embroider, with no fractional stitches and not too many colours either. Motivate your children to do embroidery from an early age. And remember, it is not only for girls. Boys also enjoy it – especially when the motif is something that tickles their fancy. Making this embroidery into a special gift contributes to its joy and value.

If you don't have moving eyes for the clown and dog, a black cross can be used in its place. Using a paper flower in the clown's hat makes it even more fun.

Be at hand to assist, if necessary, when your child does embroidery for the first time. Allow your child to choose a motif, and be patient. She will soon get the hang of it and then you won't be allowed to help anymore.

You will need

15 cm x 15 cm 6-count Aida for the clown, 15 cm x 15 cm 8-count Aida for the truck,
    5 cm x 5 cm 8-count Aida for the dog
embroidery yarn as indicated on the pattern
2 x 5 mm moving eyes for the clown, 1 x 3 mm moving eye for the dog (optional)
brightly coloured wooden frame for the clown
small cardboard box for the truck
window card for dog
fabric glue
double-sided tape

Method

1 Embroider each motif as indicated on the pattern.
2 Use 6 strands of yarn for the cross stitch and 3 strands for the back stitching.
3 Attach the moving eyes with fabric glue.

Making up

CLOWN

1 Cut the embroidered clown to the correct size to fit into the frame (see photograph page 19).

2 Stretch the embroidery neatly over the inner frame and place into the outer frame.

TRUCK

1 Frame the motif in back stitching and fray the edges.

2 Attch the embroidery to the box with double-sided tape.

DOG

Stick the embroidery into position onto a window card with double-sided tape and let your child write his own message to his gran or a favourite teacher.

More ideas

- ✕ Make a toy bag from calico and sew the clown, truck or dog onto it. The embroidery artist will most probably be more eager to tidy up when play time is over!
- ✕ Glue the embroidery onto a painted name board and attach it onto the door of your child's bedroom.

DOG

Grid Size: 16 W x 12 H
Stitches: 14 x 10

DMC	ANCHOR	DESCRIPTION
310	403	black
433	371	brown - medium
700	229	christmas green - bright

TRUCK

Grid Size: 30 W x 20 H
Stitches: 27 x 16

DMC	ANCHOR	DESCRIPTION
310	403	black
702	239	kelly green
606	335	bright orange-red
White	2	white
321	47	christmas red

CLOWN

Grid Size: 24 W x 24 H
Stitches: 21 x 20

DMC	ANCHOR	DESCRIPTION
*310	403	black
702	239	kelly green
606	335	bright orange-red
973	290	canary - bright
995	410	electric blue - dark
666	46	christmas red - light
762	397	pearl grey - very light

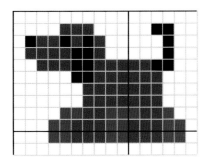

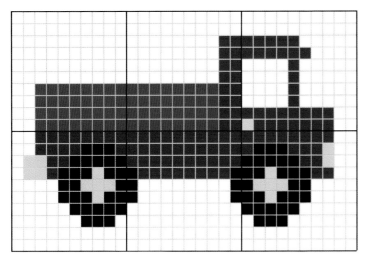

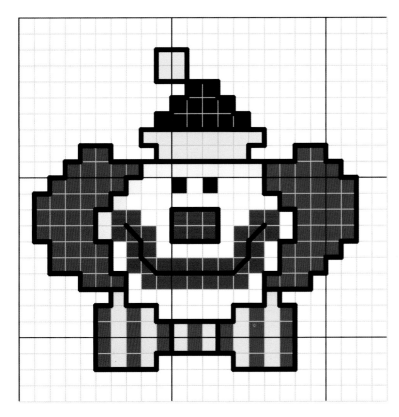

Christmas in cross stitch

Embroidering Christmas motifs is surely one of the most satisfying activities. These motifs can be used for Christmas cards, Christmas-tree decorations, on table linen, to decorate Christmas stockings, and much more.

Children, especially, look forward to Christmas with great excitement. During the festive season their sparkling eyes are reason enough to surprise them with a beautiful, unique advent calender This calender can be used year after year and your children will have many fun-filled days finding the contents of each little bag.

All the Christmas motifs for the calender were worked in metallic thread, but you can also use normal stranded cotton. The colour code with the patterns indicate normal stranded cotton. Since metallic thread is often only available in one shade of each colour, I used only one shade of red for the motifs, even though different shades of red are indicated on the pattern.

For this project I made liberal use of beads. If you prefer, you can just work cross stitches where I have used beads. Each bead represents one cross stitch and vice versa.

I used Aida for the embroidery for the calender, and even-weave for the Christmas tree decorations in the red frames. Use white, green or red, as you prefer.

You will need

10 cm x 10 cm Aida or even-weave for each motif
embroidery yarn as indicated on the pattern
red, green, gold and black beads
FOR CHRISTMAS TREE DECORATIONS
round plastic frames
white felt
fabric glue
FOR ADVENT CALENDER
double-sided tape
50 cm x 50 cm cardboard
batting
hessian to cover the cardboard
cord to glue around the tree
chocolates or small gifts (25)
fabric glue
glue gun

Method

1 Follow the pattern to embroider the motifs.
2 Use 2 strands for the cross stitch and 1 strand for the back stitching.

Making up

CHRISTMAS-TREE DECORATIONS

1 Place each embroidered motif into a frame and cut out neatly close to the edge of the frame.
2 Glue a piece of white felt to the back to finish it off neatly.

ADVENT CALENDER

1 Press a neat seam around every embroidered square and stick down with double-sided tape.
2 Draw a Christmas tree onto the cardboard and cut it out.
3 Cut the same shape out of the batting and glue to the cardboard.
4 Cover with hessian and stick down securely at the back. Cut and fold the hessian at the corners to achieve a neat finish.
5 Glue cord all around the edge of the tree to round it off.
6 Using the glue gun, apply glue to the side and bottom edges of each embroidered square and stick to the tree. Push the side edges slightly closer together towards the top so that each square forms an opening into which you can slip a chocolate or small gift.

More ideas

✗ Work beads randomly onto an embroidered Christmas tree, frame the design in back stitching and fray the edges. Using double-sided tape, glue the embroidery to a thick candle.
✗ Use the embroidered motifs to make special Christmas cards.
✗ Embroider table linen to be used for Christmas.
✗ Embellish Chistmas stockings with embroidered motifs.

ADVENT 1

Grid Size: 27 W x 27 H
Stitches: 25 x 25

DMC	ANCHOR	DESCRIPTION
300	352	mahogany - very dark
301	349	mahogany - medium
699	923	christmas green
701	227	christmas green - light
*310	403	black

Metallic thread: E669 (green), E301 (mahogany)

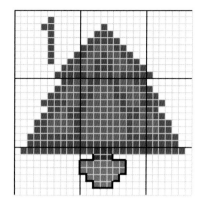

ADVENT 2

Grid Size: 20 W x 20 H
Stitches: 17 x 17

DMC	ANCHOR	DESCRIPTION
743	297	yellow - medium
*550	102	violet - very dark
307	289	lemon
333	119	blue violet - very dark

Metallic thread: E3852 (gold), E3837 (violet)

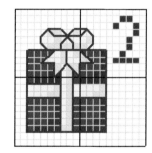

ADVENT 3

Grid Size: 20 W x 24 H
Stitches: 17 x 20

DMC	ANCHOR	DESCRIPTION
*699	923	christmas green
666	46	christmas red - bright
743	297	yellow - medium
White	2	white

Metallic thread: E699 (green), E321 (red), E3852 (gold), E5200 (white)

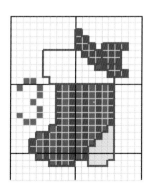

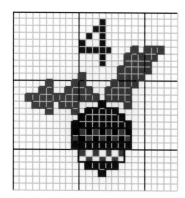

ADVENT 4

Grid Size: 25 W x 26 H
Stitches: 21 x 23

DMC	Anchor	Description
*699	923	christmas green
White	2	white
820	134	royal blue - very dark
304	47	christmas red - medium

Metallic thread: E669 (green), E321 (red), E5200 (white)

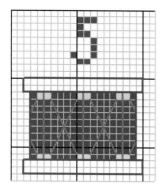

ADVENT 5

Grid Size: 22 W x 25 H
Stitches: 18 x 23

DMC	Anchor	Description
White	2	white
E3852	300	metallic gold
*909	229	emerald green-very dark
307	289	lemon

Metallic thread: E699 (green), E5200 (white)

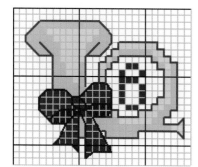

ADVENT 6

Grid Size: 27 W x 23 H
Stitches: 24 x 20

DMC	Anchor	Description
743	297	yellow - medium
307	289	lemon
304	47	christmas red - medium
321	47	christmas red
815	43	garnet - medium
*433	371	brown - medium

Metallic thread: E3852, E677 (gold), E321 (red)

ADVENT 7

Grid Size: 22 W x 26 H
Stitches: 20 x 24

DMC	Anchor	Description
700	923	christmas green - bright
743	297	yellow - medium
666	46	christmas red - bright
996	433	electric blue - medium
333	119	blue violet - very dark
*E3852	300	metallic gold
701	227	christmas green - light
340	118	blue violet - medium
304	47	christmas red - medium
*310	403	black
995	410	electric blue - dark

Metallic thread: E699 (green), E321 (red), E3843
(bright blue), E334 (light blue), E3837 (violet)

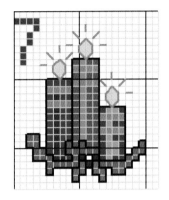

ADVENT 8

Grid Size: 25 W x 26 H
Stitches: 21 x 23

DMC	Anchor	Description
*300	352	mahogany - very dark
898	360	coffee brown - very dark
783	307	topaz - medium
321	47	christmas red
725	306	topaz
3078	292	golden yellow - very light
E3852	300	metallic gold

Metallic thread: E3821 (light gold), E168 (silver), E321 (red)

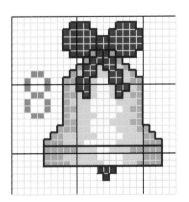

Attach gold, silver and coloured beads to the embroidered Christmas tree to look like Christmas baubles (see photograph on next page). You can also string beads and attach the strings to suggest tinsel.

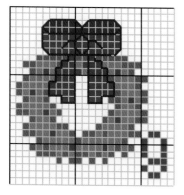

ADVENT 9

Grid Size: 25 W x 26 H

Stitches: 23 x 23

DMC	Anchor	Description
988	243	forest green - medium
987	244	forest green - dark
666	46	christmas red - bright
321	47	christmas red
498	20	garnet - dark
304	47	christmas red - medium

Metallic thread: E699, E703 (green), E321 (red)

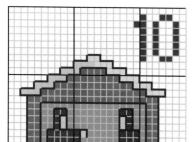

ADVENT 10

Grid Size: 27 W x 28 H

Stitches: 25 x 25

DMC	Anchor	Description
743	297	yellow - medium
841	378	beige brown - light
307	289	lemon
435	369	brown - very light
301	349	mahogany - medium
333	119	blue violet - very dark
824	164	blue - very dark
945	347	tawny - medium
300	352	mahogany - very dark

Metallic thread: E3852) (gold), E3821 (light gold), E301 (mahogany), E898 (dark brown), E3837 (violet), E3843 (blue)

ADVENT 11

Grid Size: 32 W x 31 H
Stitches: 30 x 25

DMC	ANCHOR	DESCRIPTION
310	403	black
743	297	yellow - medium
White	2	white
3747	120	blue violet - very light
321	47	christmas red
*317	400	pewter grey

Metallic thread: E321 (red), E168 (silver), E5200 (white), E3852 (gold)

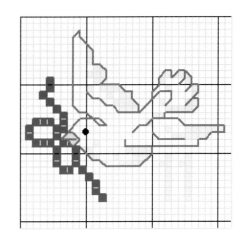

ADVENT 12

Grid Size: 24 W x 26 H
Stitches: 21 x 23

DMC	ANCHOR	DESCRIPTION
*310	403	black
White	2	white
301	349	mahogany - medium
400	351	mahogany - dark
437	362	tan - light
304	47	christmas red - medium
321	47	christmas red
760	9	salmon
*433	371	brown - medium

Metallic thread: E301 (mahogany), E677 (light gold), E321 (red)

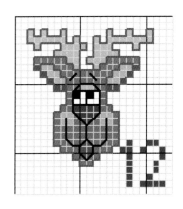

ADVENT 13

Grid Size: 22 W x 22 H
Stitches: 20 x 19

First work the back stitching in gold, then work French knots in red over the back stitching, or attach red beads instead.

DMC	ANCHOR	DESCRIPTION
726	295	topaz -light
White	2	white
321	47	christmas red
*934	862	black avocado green
*E3852	300	metallic gold
3346	257	hunter green

Metallic thread: E699 (green), E321 (red), E5200 (white)

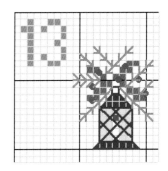

ADVENT 14

Grid Size: 25 W x 25 H

Stitches: 23 x 23

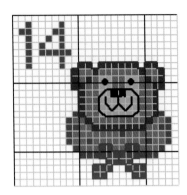

DMC	Anchor	Description
*310	403	black
702	239	kelly green
606	335	bright orange-red
*898	360	coffee brown - very dark
435	369	brown - very light
437	362	tan - light
666	46	christmas red - bright
*321	47	christmas red

Metallic thread: E301 (mahogany), E3821 (light gold), E699, E703 (green), E321 (red)

ADVENT 15

Grid Size: 18 W x 21 H

Stitches: 16 x 19

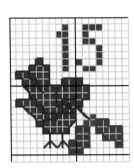

DMC	Anchor	Description
347	13	salmon - very dark
400	351	mahogany - dark
699	923	christmas green
666	46	christmas red - bright
*938	381	coffee brown - ul dark

Metallic thread: E699 (green), E301 (mahogany), E898 (dark brown), E321 (red)

ADVENT 16

Grid Size: 18 W x 27 H

Stitches: 16 x 24

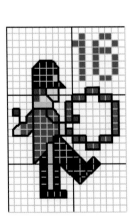

DMC	Anchor	Description
*310	403	black
820	134	royal blue - very dark
700	229	christmas green - bright
743	297	yellow - medium
Ecru	926	ecru
666	47	christmas red - bright
400	351	mahogany - dark

Metallic thread: E699 (green), E301 (mahogany), E321 (red), E3852 (gold), E677 (light gold)

ADVENT 17

Grid Size: 23 W x 28 H
Stitches: 20 x 25

DMC	Anchor	Description
*310	403	black
437	362	tan - light
702	239	kelly green
304	47	christmas red - medium
760	8	salmon
*435	42	brown - very light

Metallic thread: E699 (green), E301 (mahogany),
E321 (red), E316 (pink)

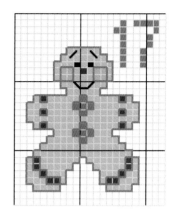

ADVENT 18

Grid Size: 21 W x 23 H
Stitches: 19 x 20

DMC	Anchor	Description
989	242	forest green
743	297	yellow - medium
321	47	christmas red
987	244	forest green - dark
*986	246	forest green - very dark
*814	44	garnet - dark

Metallic thread: E699, E703 (green), E321 (red), E3852 (gold)

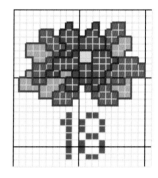

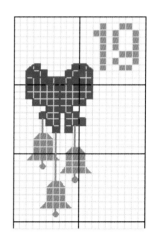

ADVENT 19

Grid Size: 20 W x 31 H
Stitches: 17 x 29

DMC	Anchor	Description
*E3852	300	metallic gold
666	46	christmas red - bright
*321	47	christmas red

Metallic thread: E321 (red)

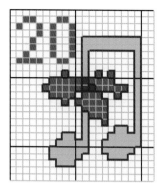

ADVENT 20

Grid Size: 22 W x 25 H

Stitches: 19 x 22

DMC	Anchor	Description
702	239	kelly green
*898	360	coffee brown - very dark
725	306	topaz
321	47	christmas red

Metallic thread: E699 (green), E321 (red), E3852 (gold)

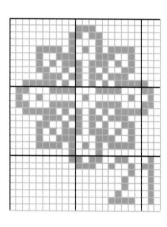

ADVENT 21

Grid Size: 23 W x 28 H

Stitches: 21 x 26

DMC	Anchor	Description
White	2	white
E168	301	metallic silver

Metallic thread: E5200 (white)

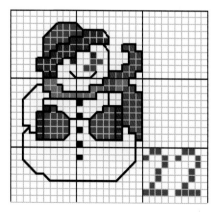

ADVENT 22

Grid Size: 30 W x 28 H

Stitches: 27 x 25

DMC	Anchor	Description
666	46	christmas red - bright
White	2	white
312	147	navy blue - light
*310	403	black
912	205	emerald green - light
910	228	emerald green - dark
498	20	christmas red - dark

Metallic thread: E699, E703 (green), E321 (red), E5200 (white)

ADVENT 23

Grid Size: 25 W x 25 H
Stitches: 22 x 22

DMC	ANCHOR	DESCRIPTION
White	2	white
*310	403	black
912	205	emerald green - light
304	47	christmas red - medium
910	228	emerald green - dark

Metallic thread: E699, E703 (green), E321 (red),
E5200 (white)

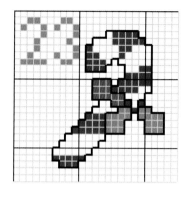

ADVENT 24

Grid Size: 25 W x 23 H
Stitches: 22 x 19

DMC	ANCHOR	DESCRIPTION
666	46	christmas red - bright
White	2	white
312	147	navy blue - light
760	8	salmon
754	778	peach - light
*310	403	black

Metallic thread: E5200 (white), E321 (red), E315 (pink)

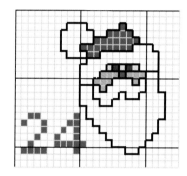

ADVENT 25

Grid Size: 20 W x 27 H
Stitches: 16 x 23

DMC	ANCHOR	DESCRIPTION
*E3852	300	metallic gold
*310	403	black
304	47	christmas red - medium
353	8	peach
435	369	brown - very light
White	2	white
553	98	violet

Metallic thread: E301 (mahogany), E321 (red),
E5200 (white), E315 (pink), E3837 (violet)

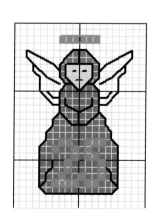

Brilliant butterfly

Use plastic canvas to make this striking trinket box decorated with a butterfly in cross stitch using the striking DMC Light Effects yarns.

The lines of the canvas are referred to as "threads" but they are not actually threads since this canvas is not woven. To cut the plastic canvas pieces accurately, count threads and not holes.

The top of the trinket box is worked in cross stitch according to the pattern, and the bottom and sides are worked in half cross stitches. Two strands are used throughout. I framed the top with a row of oblong beads, and stitched a row of the same beads in the middle of each side for an interesting finish.

Use overcast stitch to join the side and bottom sections, and place the embroidered upper section on top. The diagram for the top indicates only cross stitches, but I used beads for the body of the butterfly. Because the beads are quite big, I used only 2 beads in the place of 3 cross stitches.

For a professional finish, line the inside as well as the top of the box with felt, using double-sided tape to stick it down.

You will need

1 sheet of 14-count plastic canvas cut as follows:
    4 rectangles of 48 x 14 threads for sides
    1 square of 50 x 50 threads for the top
    1 square of 48 x 48 threads for the bottom
embroidery yarn as indicated on the pattern
22 cm x 22 cm piece of felt cut as above
double-sided tape
86 oblong beads
7 multifaceted beads

Method

1 Embroider the butterfly on the larger square as indicated on the pattern, stitching a row of oblong beads around the edges to round it off nicely.
2 Attach a row of oblong beads in the middle of each side piece, then fill in with half cross stitches.

Making up

1 Join the sides along the short edges using overcast stitch, then join the bottom to the sides using overcast stitch and cover unworked edges with overcast stitch.
2 Cut pieces of felt to fit the inside bottom and sides of the box, as well as the top, and attach with double-sided tape.

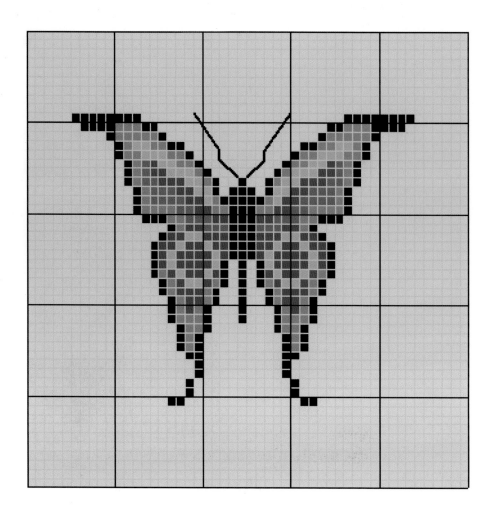

BUTTERFLY

Grid Size: 50 W x 50 H

Stitches: 50 x 50

DMC	ANCHOR	DESCRIPTION
*E 310	403	black
E 3843	1089	bright blue - medium
E 334	145	baby blue - medium
E 168	301	metallic silver
E 825	162	bright blue - dark
E 3837	98	violet
E 211	108	lavender - light